Moving Out

The Impact of Relocation from Hospital to Community on the Quality of Life of People with Learning Disabilities

---

Eric Emerson and Chris Hatton

Hester Adrian Research Centre
University of Manchester

LONDON: HMSO

CORNWALL COLLEGE
L R C

Acknowledgements

The background research and writing of this report have been supported by a grant to the Hester Adrian Research Centre from the centrally commissioned research and development programme of the English Department of Health.

An earlier (and much briefer) version of this report was presented at an international symposium on *The Dissolution of Institutions* held at the University of Uppsala, Sweden in April 1993, the proceedings of which are to be published in the near future in Mansell, J., and Ericsson, K. (Eds.) *The Dissolution of Institutions: An International Perspective*, London: Chapman & Hall. A summary of this report also appeared in the *Health Services Journal*, 19 May 1994.

We are grateful to Professor Chris Kiernan, Derek Thomas and staff of the Research and Development Division and Learning Disability Client Group at the Department of Health for helpful comments on earlier drafts of this report.

Contents

Summary

Introduction

Between 1980 and 1993 the capacity of mental handicap hospitals in the UK reduced by over 26,000 places. This change in the pattern of provision of residential services has resulted in many thousands of people with learning disabilities moving from hospital back to 'the community'. On the basis of existing plans, at least 10,000 more people in England alone will move out of long-stay mental handicap hospitals by the turn of the century.

Our intention in writing this report was to review the results of all of the research conducted in the UK since 1980 which has sought to take an objective look at the impact of these changes on the life experiences or quality of life of people with learning disabilities.

The Research Reviewed

The findings contained in this report are based upon a comprehensive review of all research studies published between 1980 and 1993 which have sought to examine the effects of the move from hospital to community on the lives of people with learning disabilities in the UK and Ireland. This included 71 publications arising from over 46 separate studies. Overall, they provided information on some aspect of the move from hospital to community on the lives of approximately 2,350 people with learning disabilities. Virtually all of the publications reviewed focused on the residential component of services received by users.

For each study we categorised the measures used in terms of general conceptualisations of the notion of quality of life and John O'Brien's idea of key service accomplishments. In addition we looked at: the staff contact provided to service users; outcomes for carers and care staff, such as satisfaction or stress experienced by care staff and the opinions of informal carers; aspects of service organisation; and service costs.

The Findings

The research evidence which we reviewed suggests that people with learning disabilities who move from larger scale institutional provision (primarily mental handicap hospitals) to smaller scale community-based services (primarily staffed houses) can, in general, expect:

- ✓ an improvement in their *material standard of living*;
- ✓ to be more *satisfied* with their services and with their life in general;
- ✓ to have more *opportunities to use skills* which they possess as well as to *develop new competencies*;
- ✓ to spend less time engaged in *stereotypic behaviours* such as rocking;
- ✓ to have more *opportunities for choice* over routine daily activities;
- ✓ to have more *contacts with other people*;
- ✓ to make more use of a greater variety of 'ordinary' *community facilities*;
- ✓ to spend more time engaged in *constructive activities*;
- ✓ to be relatively *well accepted* as customers in local businesses;
- ✓ to receive more *contact and support* from care staff;
- ✓ to be supported in a less *institutional* environment.

It is apparent, however, that these are far from inevitable consequences of the move to the community. On all measures of outcome the variation within service models was substantial. Indeed, the research suggests that for a significant minority of studies (and hence individuals) life in 'the community' would appear to be relatively indistinguishable, on these measures of outcome at least, from life in institutional provision.

The same research also suggests that, compared to the general population, people who move to community-based services can also, in general, expect to:

- ✗ remain relatively *poor*;
- ✗ develop *few new skills* once they have settled in the community;
- ✗ to continue to show more serious challenging behaviours;
- ✗ to have few, if any, *opportunities for choice* over such life defining decisions as who to live with and who to be supported by;

- × to have fewer opportunities to exercise *choice over everyday routine* matters than non-disabled people;
- × to have *few relationships with non-disabled people*, other than care staff who are paid to be with them;
- × to have little real *presence* in their communities;
- × to spend most of their day *waiting* for activities to happen or to be engaged in passive and relatively purposeless activities;
- × to receive little *active support* from staff.

Conclusions and Issues

Six general conclusions may be drawn from our review of the research evidence.

- People with learning disabilities, including those with more severe disabilities and additional needs, can be supported in the community in such a way as to significantly improve their quality of life.

- Overall, smaller community-based residential services offer a better quality of life to users than either mental handicap hospitals, medium size hostels or 'community units'.

- Community-based services vary widely in terms of their quality, to the extent that, for a significant minority of individuals, life in the community is little different from life in hospital.

- A structured approach to organising the care environment appears to be associated with consistently better outcomes, at least for people with more severe disabilities.

- There is little evidence to suggest that *within* community-based services users are developing new competencies, new relationships or extending the extent of their participation in their surrounding community.

- While more needs to be known, it does appears that the quality of life offered in many community-based services falls far short of the values and ideals which underlay their development and may also fall short of common notions of decency or acceptability when applied to non-disabled people.

Analysis of the apparent variations in quality *within* community-based residential services may, along with other evidence, indicate that the **purchasers or commissioners** of residential services will need to develop their own capacity for effectively and efficiently measuring the outcomes associated with the services they are purchasing. They may also wish to ensure that these services possess the structural and procedural characteristics which the available evidence suggests are associated with positive outcomes. This would involve assessing whether services (among other things):

- have a clear and explicit orientation or mission to provide the support to enable a *named* person or persons with learning disabilities to live and participate in the community;

- exhibit the structural characteristics appropriate to community-based services in terms of size, location, design, material resources, internal appointments and staffing requirements;

- possess and implement clearly defined procedures for ensuring the participation of users in all aspects of the running of their home;

- have clearly defined and appropriate management arrangements with regard to such issues as devolved responsibility for catering, laundry, maintenance, recruitment, purchase of provisions and materials;

- consistently implement clearly defined procedures for selecting and scheduling activities and arranging for the support necessary to enable service users to participate fully in these activities;

- have clearly defined arrangements for service users to access appropriate vocational, educational and leisure services;

- implement clearly defined and appropriate procedures for staff supervision;

- collect, on a regular basis, information concerning the quality of life experienced by the user(s) of the service.

Service **providers**, other than attending to the above requirements from purchasers, will need in particular to strengthen their capacity to effectively lead and manage dispersed semi-autonomous work groups. In addition, providers will need to pay greater attention to the development of systems for monitoring and safeguarding against the potential for abuse which exists in all types of service provision. The dispersed nature and increased visibility of community-based services present some particular challenges in this area.

In order to address some of the deficiencies noted within our review, **researchers** and those involved in local evaluations will need to:

iv

- develop ways of involving users and carers in the identification of significant outcomes;

- establish the social validity, or the social significance, of the results arising from an evaluation project, in particular by assessing the quality of life of people with learning disabilities against normative standards;

- begin to identify those individual and setting factors which may account for individual variation in people's response to the move from hospital to community;

- evaluate services on a broad range of outcomes in order to begin to identify whether different patterns of outcomes may be associated with different models of service provision;

- evaluate the outcomes associated with a broader range of approaches to residential care (e.g. supported living, village communities) in order to help ensure that more objective information is available to policy makers and those responsible for commissioning and purchasing services;

- begin to address longer-term aspects of outcomes within community-based service systems;

- attend to the development of models which seek to explain the links between service inputs, processes and outcomes;

- evaluate the outcomes associated with different models of day provision.

Introduction

Between 1980 and 1993 the capacity of mental handicap hospitals in the UK was reduced by over 26,000 places. This change in the pattern of provision of residential services has resulted in many thousands of people with learning disabilities moving from such hospitals back to 'the community'. At the time of writing, 70% of the remaining hospitals in England are scheduled for closure (Greig, 1993). When combined with the proposed reduction in size of the remaining institutions, these plans are likely to result, in England alone, in at least 10,000 more people with learning disabilities moving out of long-stay mental handicap hospitals by the turn of the century.

Our intention in writing this report is to review the results of all the research carried out in the UK since 1980 which has sought to take an objective look at the impact of these changes on the life experiences or quality of life of people with learning disabilities. The importance of standing back and taking stock of the impact of such a pervasive policy as 'care in the community' is self-evident. In this instance, however, such an exercise appears to be particularly timely.

The organisation of services for people with learning disabilities are undergoing a period of major transition resulting from the implementation of the 1990 NHS and Community Care Act. The separation of commissioning or purchasing from service provision, the enhanced role of Local Authorities and the independent sector, the introduction of new procedures for assessment and care management and new arrangements for monitoring services have all helped create new opportunities and new threats to the development of services for people with learning disabilities. More recently, the disbandment of Regional Health Authorities runs the risk of taking away from the NHS some of the key leadership which has played a significant role in bringing about a co-ordinated approach to hospital closure (Korman and Glennerster, 1990). As people take up the new positions created by these changes they will need access to up to date information concerning the effectiveness and impact of policy changes. It is our hope that this report will meet some of their needs.

Standing back and taking a dispassionate view of the effects of the phase down or closure of mental handicap hospitals is also particularly important given the intensity of the debate which has, and continues to, surround this policy. While few would advocate retaining institutional provision in its current form, strong opinions continue to be voiced regarding the need for some form of institutional provision for people with more complex needs (e.g. Segal, 1990). Indeed, the process of hospital closure has always been highly politicised. Professionals, managers and researchers have made extensive personal investment in advocating for particular models of care. Indeed, for some, reputations and careers are based upon the purported success (or lack thereof) of the deinstitutionalisation movement in general or on the presumed superiority of particular approaches to the development of community-based services. An obvious danger exists that those of us who have been closely involved in this process will come to accept the rhetoric, rather than investigate the reality, of the policy options in question.

Finally, the early identification of 'care in the community' with hospital *closure* or deinstitutionalisation has unwittingly encouraged a belief that, as this specific task is nearing completion, attention (and resources) may usefully be diverted to competing priorities on the social agenda, including, for example, media and public opposition to the closure of psychiatric hospitals. As such, it would appear particularly timely to take a hard look at the successes and failures of the hospital closure programme.

It is, of course, rather inappropriate to talk of the hospital closure programme as if it were some homogeneous entity. There have been, and remain, significant variations over time and across countries, regions and localities in the ways in which these policies have been implemented. The phasing out of mental handicap hospitals began earlier and has proceeded on a more widespread basis in England than in Wales, Scotland or Northern Ireland. Thus, by 1992 the English institutional population had dropped to 44% of its 1980 level, with proportionally larger institutional populations remaining in Wales (53%), Scotland (57%) and Northern Ireland (70%). The accelerating pace of the reduction in size of hospital-based provision for people with learning disabilities in England is illustrated in Figure 1[1], which shows the year-on-year institutional populations for the four home countries expressed as a percentage of the corresponding institutional population in 1980.

Similarly, the nature of the services developed in the community to replace hospital provision has varied over time and across locations. Very generally, the first wave of deinstitutionalisation in the UK involved the move of those individuals with the least severe disabilities to a range of often pre-existing services including hostels, semi-supported group homes, family placement schemes, bed and breakfast

---

[1] The discontinuity in the data results from a change in the Department of Health's approach to the collection of hospital statistics during 1987.

arrangements and independent living (Korman and Glennerster, 1990; Malin, 1987). During the 1980's, however, attention switched to the development of community-based residential provision for people with more severe disabilities, including those with additional needs such as sensory impairments or 'challenging' behaviour (Blunden and Allen, 1987; Department of Health and Social Security, 1984; Department of Health, 1989, 1993).

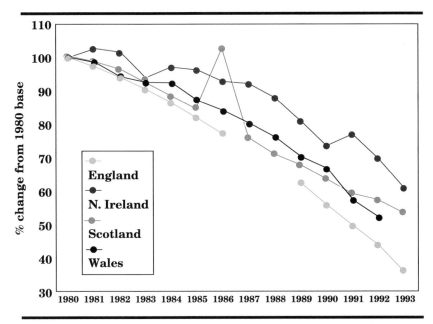

Figure 1: *NHS Mental Handicap Hospital places in the UK 1980-1993*

Thinking about what may constitute the most appropriate alternative to hospital services for people with more severe disabilities has itself undergone some significant changes. Initial developments focused on the establishment of purpose built 20-24 place 'locally-based hospital' or 'community' units to serve a defined geographical area (e.g. Felce et al, 1980; Simon, 1981). During the mid-1980's, however, these ideas gave way (at least in most areas) to an interest in developing services based on the provision of staff support to people with severe disabilities within smaller domestic scale 'ordinary' housing (Felce, 1989; Lowe and de Paiva, 1991; Mansell et al, 1987). More recently, the appropriateness of this 'staffed housing' model has itself been questioned by calls for the development of 'supported living' arrangements which seek to place the person with disabilities at the very centre of service planning and organisation (Kinsella, 1993; O'Brien, 1994).

The causes underlying these changes in conceptions of what constitutes the most appropriate form of community-based residential provision for people with severe disabilities are undoubtably complex.

One particularly significant factor, however, has been the extent to which these changes, or at least the rhetoric surrounding them, have been influenced by the concepts of normalisation and social role valorization (Emerson, 1992; Nirje, 1992; Wolfensberger, 1992) and, in particular, the ways these ideas have been elaborated by John O'Brien (e.g. O'Brien, 1987; O'Brien and Tyne, 1981) and disseminated in an influential series of working parties organised by the King's Fund (Blunden and Allen, 1987; King's Fund, 1980, 1984, 1989). Indeed, many of the notions underlying these concepts have come to be reflected in statements of local, regional and national policy (e.g. Department of Health, 1989; Guy's Health District, 1981; North Western Regional Health Authority, 1983).

In the following pages we will summarise the results of the research undertaken in the UK since 1980 which has examined the impact of relocation from mental handicap hospitals to community-based services on the quality of life and lifestyle of people with learning disabilities. Our decision to focus solely upon research conducted in the UK does not mean, of course, that some important general lessons cannot be learned from the experiences of deinstitutionalisation in other countries (e.g. Anninson and Young, 1980; Bank-Mikkelsen, 1980; Bruininks and Lakin, 1985; Bruininks et al, 1981; Butler and Bjaanes, 1983; Emerson, 1985; Haney, 1988; Jacobsen and Schwartz, 1991; Janicki et al, 1988; Nisbet et al, 1991). Rather, it reflects our belief that the specific form in which this general policy has been transacted will be considerably influenced by aspects of local policy, service infrastructure and culture. Care needs to be taken when adopting a pan-cultural approach to the evaluation of the impact of seemingly similar social policies.

Before summarising the results of UK research, however, we will briefly describe our approach in undertaking this review.

The Review Process

The findings contained in this report are based upon a comprehensive review of all research studies which have been published since 1980 and which have sought to examine the effects of the move from hospital to community on the lives of people with learning disabilities in the UK.

Studies were identified through a combination of computer-based searches of on-line databases (Social Sciences Citation Index and PsycLit), following up references cited in published reports and discussion with active researchers in the UK. Studies were included in the review if they:

- provided quantitative or qualitative information on any aspect of the quality of life or lifestyle of service users in either hospital or community based residential or day care, or

- involved evaluations of the deinstitutionalisation process itself.

This process identified 71 publications from over 46 separate studies. Overall, they provided information on some aspect of the move from hospital to community on the lives of approximately 2,350 people with learning disabilities. Virtually all of the studies we reviewed focused solely on the residential component of services received by users. Details of the 71 publications reviewed are contained in an Appendix.

Types of Services

As we noted in the introduction, significant changes occurred during the 1980's with regard to the nature of community-based residential alternatives to hospital care. Not surprisingly, these changes are reflected in the types of services which have been evaluated. Figure 2, below, shows a breakdown by year of publication and type of service evaluated for the 71 publications included in the review. To enable comparisons to be made in the review we divided services into one of four categories:

- mental handicap *hospitals*;
- *hostels/units*, which included all examples of Local Authority run hostels, newly built 'community units', 'locally-based hospital units' and recently established specialised NHS operated units developed on the grounds of existing institutional provision;
- *staffed houses*, which included all examples of services in which 24 hour staff support was provided in 'ordinary' domestic-scale housing;
- *other*, which included those few examples of independent living or family placement schemes which have been evaluated.

Two trends are apparent from inspection of Figure 2. Firstly, the numbers of research studies published has gradually increased over the period reviewed. Secondly, the majority of particularly more recent studies have looked at comparisons between mental handicap hospitals and community-based staffed housing.

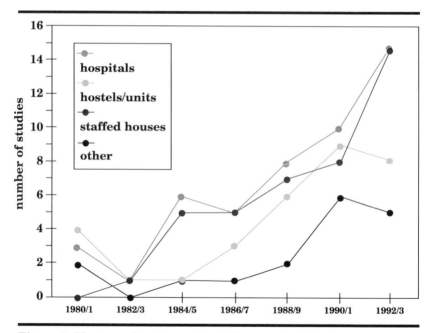

Figure 2: *The types of services evaluated by year of publication*

We examined in greater detail those studies which examined directly the effects of moving from:

- *hospitals to hostels/units* (20 studies involving approximately 650 service users);
- *hospitals to staffed houses* (34 studies; 1,200 users);
- *hostels/units to staffed houses* (9 studies; 100 users).

Service Users

A breakdown of the degree of disability, age and gender of the 2,350 service users participating in these studies is provided below in Table 1.

Table 1: *Age, Gender and Level of Disability of Participants*

Gender	men	59%
	women	41%
Age	children	6%
	adults	74%
	unspecified	20%
Level of Learning Disability	mild/moderate	16%
	severe/profound	33%
	mixed	31%
	unspecified	20%

Three factors combine to make judgements regarding the representativeness of this sample problematic. These are:

- the scant information provided in many studies;

- the paucity of information regarding the characteristics of people with learning disabilities in the UK as a whole;

- the paucity of information regarding the characteristics of people with learning disabilities who are either currently resident in or have moved out of mental handicap hospitals.

We believe it can safely be assumed, however, that, as a result of selective processes operating on hospital admission and discharge (e.g. age, presence of challenging behaviour, severity of disability), the participants of the reviewed studies will not be representative of the British population of people with learning disabilities. The extent to which they are representative of the group of people with learning disabilities who have moved out of hospital since 1980 is less clear.

Summarising Outcomes

Not surprisingly, the 71 publications included in the review took very different approaches to measuring the impact of hospital and community-based care on the life experiences or quality of life of service users. In an attempt to bring some order to this diversity, the measures of outcome used in the individual studies were categorised according to a number of general domains. These included two sets of outcome measures traditionally linked to the evaluation of quality of life in the general social science literature (c.f. Emerson, 1985; Felce and Perry, in press; Parmenter, 1992; Schalock, 1990):

- *social indicators* of the material aspects of an individual's quality of life, for example disposable income (e.g. Walker et al, 1993), aspects of the physical environment provided by services (e.g. Felce et al, 1985) and the numbers and types of personal possessions held by service users (e.g. Davies, 1988);

- *user satisfaction* with regards to their overall quality of life (e.g. Stanley and Roy, 1988) and with the services they receive (e.g. Knapp et al, 1992).

In addition, outcome measures were categorised in terms of John O'Brien's notion of key service accomplishments, a framework closely related to the concepts of normalisation and social role valorization (Emerson, 1992). These key service accomplishments seek to define aspects of the 'lifestyle' of service users which would be closely related to the extent to which services successfully implemented the ideas of normalisation and/or social role valorization. These are:

- the *competence* or *personal growth* in skills and abilities of service users (e.g. Lowe and de Paiva, 1991), including changes in *challenging behaviours* shown by service users (e.g. Mansell and Beasley, 1993);

- *opportunities for choice* available to service users (e.g. Cattermole et al, 1988);

- the participation of users in *relationships* with family, friends and acquaintances (e.g. Malin, 1982; Markova et al, 1992);

- the *presence* of service users in the community and their participation in community-based activities (e.g. de Kock et al, 1988), including the *engagement* or participation of service users in everyday activities (e.g. Felce et al, 1980, 1986a);

- the *status* of service users and their *acceptance* by the local community (e.g. McConkey et al, 1993).

Due to the amount of information available on changes in challenging behaviour and user engagement in on-going activities, these two areas will be dealt with separately within the main body of the report.

Finally, we also summarised information pertaining to:

- the *staff contact* provided to service users (e.g. Orlowska et al, 1991);

- *outcomes for carers and care staff*, such as satisfaction or stress experienced by care staff (e.g. Emerson et al, 1993) and the opinions of informal carers (Walker et al, 1993);

- aspects of *service organisation* (e.g. Hewson and Walker, 1992);

- service *costs* (e.g. Shiell et al, 1992).

Figure 3 gives a breakdown of the numbers of studies which included outcome measures in each of these domains

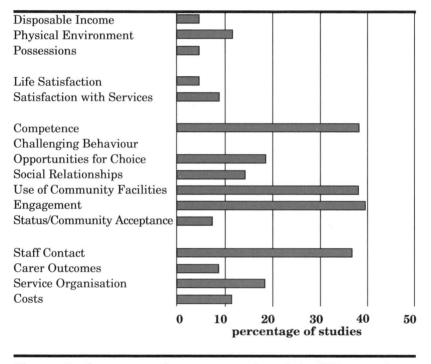

Figure 3: *Outcomes and processes evaluated in UK research on deinstitutionalisation 1980-1993*

As is readily apparent, the bulk of the evaluation literature has focused on three main domains: user engagement in ongoing activities; user participation in community-based activities; and the competencies or abilities of users. Overall, the publications reviewed reported an average of three outcome domains per study, with only 15 publications reporting information on five or more outcome domains. With such a restriction of outcome measures used by evaluation studies, it is clearly not feasible to reliably identify differing patterns of outcomes characteristic of particular service models. However, by summarising data on individual outcome domains across service models, some overall picture of the impact of different service models on the quality of life of people with learning disabilities can be drawn.

For each study the results relating to each of the outcome measures used were categorised as reflecting

- a significant improvement,

- no change, or

- a significant deterioration

on the move from the *more* institutional to the *less* institutional setting. This was done on the basis of either the study reporting a *statistically significant difference* between the two types of services or, for three purely qualitative studies, the presence of an *unqualified and unambiguous statement* concerning differences between the service models.

It should be stressed that this strategy is based upon the identification of group change. It is, of course, possible that an overall result of 'no change' may reflect marked variation in responses to change among individual participants. Similarly, a positive outcome may be achieved even though not everyone in the group showed a similar pattern of change. As yet, however, the research conducted in this area has largely failed to address the issue of identifying those individual and setting factors which may account for individual variation in people's response to the move from hospital to community

For the purposes of this review, comparison group studies and longitudinal studies comparing different models of service provision were pooled, since the findings of comparison group and longitudinal designs were very similar. Given the short-term nature of the bulk of the longitudinal studies reviewed, this similarity is unsurprising, and findings from more long-term longitudinal studies will be discussed separately where appropriate.

The Effects of Relocation

In the following pages we will present the findings of our review for each of the domains listed in the previous section. Where appropriate, we have also provided a quantitative summary of the results across studies.

Quality of Life

Social Indicators

Social indicators are those measurable 'objective' indices which, by consensus, are thought to be associated with a better quality of life. They are commonly used in the social sciences to measure the quality of life provided in different countries, regions or cities, or the quality of life experienced by different groups within society. They include such factors as physical health, access to health care, quality of housing, years of education, employment status and disposable income.

Given their widespread use elsewhere, it is rather surprising that only ten of the studies reviewed employed social indicators to evaluate aspects of the quality of life of service users.

- Two studies reported that users in community-based staffed houses had more *disposable income* than users in hospitals. However, actual levels of disposable income varied widely depending on district funding arrangements (Davies, 1988; Walker et al, 1993), with the majority of people living independently receiving very little income (Flynn, 1989).

- Seven studies examined some aspect of the *physical environment* of the settings in which service users lived. This usually involved the use of rating scales to determine how 'normalised' the user's home was (e.g. Beswick, 1992; Conneally et al, 1992) or the general quality of the physical environment (e.g. Cullen et al, in press; Felce et al, 1985). Not surprisingly, these studies tended to find that community-based services are more 'normalised' than hospital settings, and that the quality of the physical environment in community-based settings is higher than that in hospital settings.

11

Some studies also highlighted, however, the relatively poor state of repair of community-based residential services (e.g. Flynn, 1989; Sinson, 1990).

- Two studies investigated the number of *personal possessions* owned by users in different types of services (Booth et al, 1990; Conneally et al, 1992). Both reported that users in community-based service settings own more personal possessions than service users in hospital settings.

- Finally, one study (Flynn, 1989) outlined the *employment status* of people with learning disabilities living independently. Only 14% of people were in open employment, with 31% of people unemployed and looking for work.

Although the number of studies is small, they do present a very consistent picture of service users having a materially better quality of life in terms of having more disposable income, more personal possessions and living in better physical conditions in community-based services compared to mental handicap hospitals.

While this picture is generally encouraging (although not unsurprising), the research from which it is drawn has three important limitations. Firstly, some of the measures (particularly the normalisation rating scales) are almost guaranteed to show improvements in community-based housing services compared to hospitals, since many items are concerned with how closely the physical environment approximates to 'normal' living conditions. Secondly, the range of social indicators used has been fairly narrow, and has failed to encompass other indicators (e.g. overcrowding, access to health care) which may give a broader picture of the quality of life of people with learning disabilities. Thirdly, studies using social indicators have generally only provided comparisons across different services for people with learning disabilities. As such, they have failed to provide comparisons between the quality of life of people with learning disabilities and the general population. If one of the aims of the policy of 'care in the community' is to enable people with severe disabilities to experience a quality of life commensurate with the rest of society (c.f. Tossebro, 1993), then such comparisons are necessary if the success of this aim is to be evaluated (c.f. Emerson, 1985).

User Satisfaction

Seven of the reviewed studies evaluated either users' satisfaction with the services they were receiving or their satisfaction with life in general. Given the generally acknowledged importance of listening to the views of the consumers of our services and the weak relationship between 'objective' indicators of quality of life and expressed life satisfaction, it is somewhat surprising that such a low proportion of studies have sought to elicit the views of service users. This cannot be wholly accounted for by the severity of disability of the participants in the studies.

The majority of studies which have sought to evaluate the levels of satisfaction of service users have employed qualitative interviewing techniques to explore both satisfaction with services and life in general (e.g. Flynn, 1989; Jahoda et al, 1990; Walker et al, 1993), others have used more structured interviews (e.g. Knapp et al, 1992). One study relied solely on information gained by interviewing care staff (Stanley and Roy, 1988).

Overall, studies have reported a general improvement in user satisfaction with services associated with moves from mental handicap hospitals to community-based services (Knapp et al, 1992; Walker et al, 1993), although it is apparent that such an improvement in satisfaction with services is not inevitable (Clare and Murphy, 1993; Jahoda et al, 1990). Studies also report similar improvements in satisfaction with lifestyle and life in general (Beswick, 1992; Cullen et al, in press; Knapp et al, 1992; Stanley and Roy, 1988).

While, again, the overall results of these studies are encouraging, they are subject to a number of methodological and conceptual limitations. Firstly, many of the studies require users to compare their current community-based service with their previous stay in a mental handicap hospital. Such a procedure is clearly susceptible to both the biasing effects of memory and to social desirability effects, ie. the tendency of informants to report what they think the interviewer wants to hear. Secondly, satisfaction with services and lifestyle is often conceptualised relatively narrowly and assessed using only one method. Little consideration has been given to the multi-dimensional nature of satisfaction with life and the multiple methods required to capture its complexity (c.f. Felce and Perry, in press; Knapp et al, 1992). Finally, all but one study only compared expressed life satisfaction within groups of service users, rather than comparing the satisfaction of life reported by service users to the satisfaction of life reported by people without learning disabilities in their local communities. The one exception (Stanley and Roy, 1988) unfortunately relied upon staff reports of users' satisfaction with life, severely limiting the utility of the study. As noted above, if the aim of our services is to enable users to experience a quality of life commensurate with the rest of society, then comparing satisfaction with hospitals to satisfaction with small scale domestic housing is simply asking the wrong question.

Lifestyle

Competence & Personal Growth

Increasing the competence, abilities and skills of people with learning disabilities or enabling them to 'maximise their potential' provided one of the most important rationales during the early stages of the replacement of mental handicap hospitals with smaller community-based forms of residential care. Early evaluation research, in North America in particular, reflected this ethos with the 'success' of deinstitutionalisation being almost solely defined in terms of the rate with which users developed new skills. While our conceptualisation of the aims of 'care in the community' have progressed, the measurement of personal growth among service users continues to be emphasised in research.

Twenty-six of the studies reviewed examined some aspect of the personal competence of service users, primarily through the use of questionnaires and rating scales completed by care staff (e.g. Fleming and Stenfert Kroese, 1990; Locker et al, 1984; Lowe and de Paiva, 1990; Martindale and Kilby, 1982). While these studies have almost exclusively defined personal competence in terms of adaptive behaviour and personal skills rather than IQ, the measures used to assess adaptive behaviour have varied widely across studies. The most common measure of personal competence used by these studies is the Adaptive Behavior Scale (Part I) (Nihira et al, 1974), used by nine studies. Other measures included the Pathways To Independence Checklist (Jeffree and Cheseldine, 1982), the Schedule of Handicaps, Behaviour and Skills (Wing and Gould, 1979), the Disability Assessment Schedule (Holmes et al, 1982), the Vineland Social Maturity Scale (Doll, 1953; Sparrow et al, 1984), Progress Assessment Charts (Gunzburg, 1968, 1974), the Social Training Achievement Record (Williams, 1986), the Behavior Development Scale (Conroy, 1980) and the Potential Development Index (Toogood, 1974). Several studies (e.g. Cullen et al, in press; Knapp et al, 1992; Walker et al, 1993) have either developed individual scales or combined items from several different existing scales. Only one study (Cullen et al, in press), has used information from service users themselves in assessing personal competence.

Of the 26 studies which assessed personal competence, 21 of them included 24 separate comparisons of user competence across different types of services (e.g. Felce et al, 1986b). The results of these comparisons are summarised below in Figure 4[2].

---

[2] This and all subsequent figures are based on the number of comparisons made within studies which, due to some studies involving comparisons between more than two types of service model, may be greater than the number of studies quoted. The numbers at the top of each column of this and all subsequent figures indicate the total number of participants across all studies with that particular outcome.

14

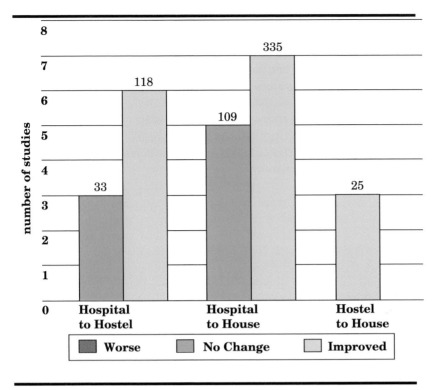

Figure 4: *Change in the competencies of service users across different types of services*

As can be seen, while the majority of studies reported an increase in personal competence associated with the *move* to smaller community-based residential provision (67% of moves from hospital to hostel; 58% hospital to house), a significant proportion of studies (33% overall) reported no significant differences in personal competence across the different models of care. Clearly, the provision of community-based housing per se is not sufficient to guarantee growth in the personal competence of service users.

The use of standardised measures to evaluate the competencies, skills and abilities of service users does mean, of course, that some information is available concerning the reliability and validity of the data obtained. Unfortunately, however, this information is often gathered from institutionalised samples of service users in North America. Studies of deinstitutionalisation in the UK have rarely taken the trouble to independently evaluate the reliability and/or validity of the measures employed. This does have a number of rather problematic consequences for the interpretation of the results of such studies.

Firstly, lack of knowledge concerning the inter-rater reliability of the scales (ie. the extent to which different members of staff would complete the questionnaires in the same way) does place some considerable limitations on their interpretation. This is more than an academic point as those studies which have evaluated the effects of moving from hospital

15

to the community have typically collected their information from two distinct sets of staff groups. Staff groups employed in the closing institutions and the newly established community-based services are likely to differ in relation to such factors as age, qualifications, work experience, training, values and attitudes (Allen et al, 1990). It is certainly possible that such differences may have the effect of biasing the responses of staff to questions regarding the abilities of service users. This leaves open the possibility that increased scores on adaptive behaviour scales may reflect differences in staff expectations rather than differences in the abilities of service users.

Secondly, it is questionable whether any (reliable) results on such scales actually reflect an increase in the competence of service users. The majority of scales used to measure changes in 'adaptive behaviours' contain items which assume that the user has access to a range of activities associated with living in the community (e.g. use of public transport, shops, banks). Clearly, users living in hospital are less likely to experience such activities on anything like a regular basis. As a result, it is possible that those studies which report increases in the competencies of service users in community-based settings may actually be reflecting the increased opportunity for users to display the competencies which they already possess in the community. This does suggest that adaptive behaviour scales may be more accurately thought of as a composite measure of two aspects of service user quality of life:

- the repertoire of competencies which a service user has available for use;

- the environmental opportunities available for the display of a service user's competencies.

Such a re-conceptualisation of the meaning of the results of adaptive behaviour scales is supported by two observations. Firstly, many studies report greater increases in skills in those areas where increased opportunities to display them are more likely to be available in community settings (such as domestic activity), and smaller increases in skills in those areas where opportunities to display them are available in both hospital and community settings (such as social skills) (e.g. Fleming and Stenfert Kroese, 1990; Walker et al, 1993). Secondly, those few studies which have evaluated changes in the personal competence of service users over several years (e.g. Cambridge et al, 1993; Hemming, 1986; Lowe et al, 1993) have tended to report a 'plateau effect', in which large initial gains resulting from the move to community-based services are followed by few additional gains once service users are living within community-based services. Such studies strongly suggest that increases in adaptive behaviours reflect the increased opportunities available to service users in community settings, rather than the continued development of the competence, skills and abilities of service users over time.

Challenging Behaviours

One parallel aspect of the growth in the general competence of service users is the extent to which they show less evidence of 'challenging behaviours'. These are culturally unusual or unacceptable behaviours such as self-injury or aggression which place the health or safety of the person or others in jeopardy or are likely to lead to the person being excluded from or denied access to ordinary community settings. The effects of relocation from hospital to community on the challenging behaviour of service users is particularly important given the recent debate concerning the viability of providing community-based services for all people with learning disabilities, including those with severely challenging behaviours (e.g. Blunden and Allen, 1987; Department of Health, 1989, 1993; Department of Health and Social Security, 1984).

Two complementary approaches have been taken to evaluating the relationship between models of service provision and changes in the extent and nature of challenging behaviours shown by service users. The majority of studies (involving 14 comparisons) evaluated change in challenging behaviour through the use of standardised rating scales which are used to solicit information from key informants such as care staff (e.g. Murphy and Clare, 1991). Scales used included Part II of the Adaptive Behavior Scale (Nihira et al, 1974), the problem behaviour sections of the Schedule of Handicaps, Behaviour and Skills (Wing and Gould, 1979) and the Disability Assessment Schedule (Holmes et al, 1982), and challenging behaviour assessment measures developed for individual studies (Hewson and Walker, 1992; Hoefkens and Allen, 1990).

A smaller number of studies (involving 11 separate comparisons) directly observed service users over varying periods of time to measure changes in the amount of time users exhibited challenging behaviours (e.g. Emerson et al, 1993). The results arising from these two approaches are summarised in Figures 5 and 6.

As can be seen, the two approaches taken to measuring challenging behaviour give very different results. The use of rating scales to obtain information from third parties indicates that the move from more to less institutional settings is associated with no change in the challenging behaviours shown by users (64% or 9 out of 14 comparisons). For a significant minority (43%; 3/7) of comparisons between hospitals and staffed housing, this approach resulted in the reporting of a significant *increase* in challenging behaviours on moving to smaller community-based services.

In contrast, those studies which directly observed service users reported an overall reduction in challenging behaviour associated with the move to community-based services, although this was only the case for 43% (3/7) of comparisons between hospital-based provision and small community-based staffed housing.

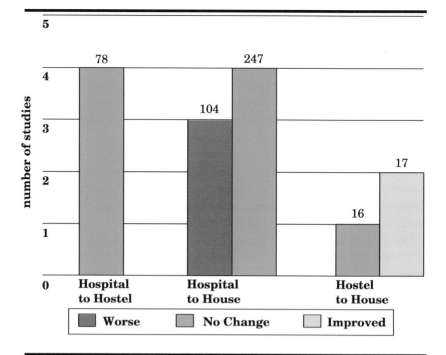

Figure 5: *Change in reported levels of challenging behaviours shown by users across different types of services*

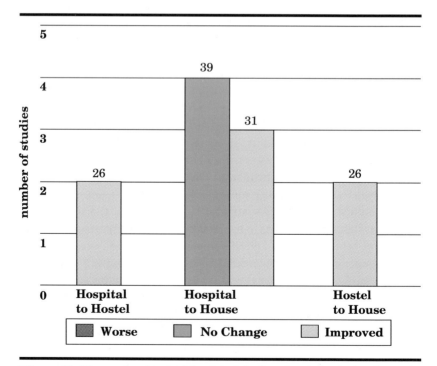

Figure 6: *Change in observed levels of challenging behaviours shown by users across different types of services*

A number of factors may account for these discrepancies. Firstly, as noted above, the replacement of hospital-based care with small scale domestic housing projects has most commonly involved the appointment and training of new staff groups rather than the transfer of both staff and users. As such, any changes in staff reports across settings may reflect either changes in the behaviour of users or the attitudes and expectations of informants towards the behaviour of users. This may be particularly significant given the use of 'values-based' training to raise the expectations of primarily inexperienced and unqualified support staff in community based-services (cf. Towell, 1988; Towell and Beardshaw, 1991). Such changes in expectations may be plausibly linked to staff in community-based services showing reduced tolerance for some forms of challenging behaviour.

Secondly, the opportunity for and social consequences of certain forms of challenging behaviour may vary between hospital and community. At a very basic level, enriched material environments are likely to provide greater opportunity for destructive behaviours. In addition, behaviours which may have relatively insignificant social consequences in hospital (e.g. 'posting' objects out of an upstairs window) are likely to prove more challenging in a terraced house.

Finally, the discrepancies between the approaches to measurement may reflect differential sensitivity to change among particular forms of challenging behaviour. Thus, for example, observational measures which are most commonly based on estimating the amount of time users spend engaged in particular behaviours are likely to be more sensitive to changes in behaviours which occur for significant proportions of time (e.g. stereotypic behaviours such as rocking and hand waving) than behaviours which may be relatively infrequent and brief but nonetheless challenging (e.g. aggression, self-injury). Interview-based approaches, however, are likely to sample a wider range of behaviours, including those less frequent, brief but intense behaviours such as aggression which staff may well find challenging.

While there is ample evidence that stereotypic behaviours may diminish in more enriched environments (e.g. Horner, 1980), there is little evidence to suggest that this relationship holds true for more seriously challenging behaviours. Indeed, there exists accumulating evidence that, while the motivational bases underlying seriously challenging behaviours are undoubtably complex and diverse (Murphy, 1994), social avoidance and escape from carer mediated demands appear to underlie many examples of severe self-injurious and aggressive behaviours (e.g. Derby et al, 1992; Emerson, 1990). As such, it would be expected that, all other things being equal, a move to more enriched environments in which users are expected to participate in the activities of an 'ordinary life' would be associated with an increase in such forms of severe challenging behaviour.

Whichever of these explanations is the most plausible, it is clear that the evidence indicates that, with the exception of stereotypic behaviour, the move from hospital to community is certainly not necessarily associated with any reductions in the challenging behaviour shown by service users. On the other hand, there is now also extensive evidence from demonstration projects that people with even the most severe challenging behaviour can be successfully cared for in small community-based services (Emerson and McGill, 1993; Felce et al, 1994).

Opportunities for Choice

The ideas of choice and the empowerment of service users are central to the more recent developments in community-based services (e.g. Department of Health, 1989; Kinsella, 1993). Twelve of the studies included in the review contained some consideration of the opportunities for choice available to service users across different types of services. Methods used for evaluating opportunities for choice varied widely, and included:

- qualitative interviews with service users (e.g. Cattermole et al, 1988; Flynn, 1989), families (Walker et al, 1993) and staff (e.g. Dockrell et al, 1993);

- quantitative scales rated by staff, such as the Personal Independence, Services and Management Schedule (Wing et al, 1985; used by Beswick, 1992) and the Quality of Life Questionnaire (Cragg and Harrison, 1984; used by Donegan and Potts, 1988);

- physical indicators assumed to correspond with service user choice, such as restrictions on service user access to various areas of living environments (Felce et al, 1985) and the amount of time service users' living environments were locked (Murphy et al, 1991).

Studies using a loose definition of autonomy and choice have typically reported improvements in autonomy and choice in community settings compared to hospitals (e.g. Dockrell et al, 1993; McHatton et al, 1988). Studies focusing on autonomy and choice over daily activities have also reported a general improvement associated with moves to community settings (e.g. Beswick, 1992; Felce et al, 1985), although there is some evidence that opportunities for autonomy and choice may be restricted for service users compared to the general population (Fleming and Stenfert Kroese, 1990). Studies concerning service user choice over important life decisions, such as where to move to and who to move with when being resettled from a hospital, and what the user's service package should contain, report service users as having little choice over these aspects of their lives (Cattermole et al, 1988; Walker et al, 1993), although Flynn (1989) did report that people's living arrangements mostly reflected their active preferences.

The variety of methods used to evaluate service user autonomy and choice reflect a lack of conceptual agreement about what aspects of choice are important and how they are to be investigated. However, two aspects of service user autonomy and choice emerge from these studies as of potential importance. The first concerns the opportunities for service users to exercise choice over daily activities, which seem to be generally improved in community settings compared to institutions, although, as noted above, such opportunities may be restricted for service users compared to the general population (Fleming and Stenfert Kroese, 1990). The second concerns the opportunities for service users to exercise choice over more substantial life decisions, which do not at present seem to be readily available to service users. While rhetoric concerning the empowerment of service users is commonplace within services, it is readily apparent that there is yet some substantial way to go before service users have any real control over important aspects of their lives.

Relationships

Ten of the studies included in the review investigated some aspect of the nature of the social relationships which occur between service users and others. Two methods have been commonly used to explore this issue: the completion of diaries by carers detailing the frequency of contacts between service users and their family and friends (e.g. de Kock et al, 1988; Fleming and Stenfert Kroese, 1990); and interviews conducted with service users (e.g. Cattermole et al, 1988; Flynn, 1989; Malin, 1982) or with relatives (Walker et al, 1993) concerning the quantity and quality of service users' social relationships.

Again, the relative dearth of studies exploring this issue makes a summary of findings tentative, but the two methods employed have produced largely consistent results. Firstly, those studies which have examined the frequency of contact between service users, friends and relatives have generally reported an increase in the frequency of social contacts in community settings compared to hospitals (e.g. Beswick, 1992; de Kock et al, 1988; Lowe and de Paiva, 1991). They have also reported, however, that the frequency of such contact, particularly with people who are not other residents, staff or relatives, remains very low in community settings (e.g. Cattermole et al, 1988; Fleming and Stenfert Kroese, 1990; Knapp et al, 1992; Lowe and de Paiva, 1991). Those studies which have examined the depth of social relationships have reported that relationships with people without learning disabilities outside the family are either superficial or generally non-existent (e.g. Cattermole et al, 1988; Jahoda et al, 1990; Walker et al,

1993). It is also worth noting that increased contact with people in local communities is not necessarily positive. Flynn (1989) reports that, while 43% of people living independently had regular contact with neighbours, many people reported this contact as negative in character.

Thus, the available evidence suggests that, while social contacts may be richer in community-based services, people with learning disabilities continue to have the bulk of their relationships with other people with disabilities or paid staff. Contact with non-disabled members of the community remains infrequent and superficial.

Community Presence

The presence of people with disabilities in community settings and their participation in community-based activities is often seen as the foundation for their true social integration. Twenty of the studies included in the review contained comparisons between types of services with regard to the extent to which service users participated in community-based activities. Most commonly, these studies assessed the use of community-based facilities (e.g. banks, shops, cinemas) either retrospectively through interviews with care staff (e.g. Dockrell et al, 1993) and/or service users (e.g. Jahoda et al, 1990; Malin, 1982), or prospectively using some form of diary completed by care staff (eg, Bratt and Johnston, 1988; de Kock et al, 1988; Evans et al, 1985; Fleming and Stenfert Kroese, 1990). One study (McConkey et al, 1993) interviewed neighbours of service users living in community-based staffed housing regarding the amount of contact they had with service users.

As can be seen in Figure 7, while the majority of comparisons (66% overall) reported a significant increase in the use of community-based facilities in smaller community-based settings, a minority of studies (31%), including 36% of comparisons between hospitals and community-based staffed housing, reported no such change. One study (Hemming et al, 1981) reported significantly less use of community based facilities in staffed houses located on a hospital site when compared with mental handicap hospital wards.

Although some caution must be expressed when interpreting these results, due to concerns about the reliability of both diary data (Joyce et al, 1989) and retrospective interview data, the set of studies reviewed provide a relatively coherent picture of increased user participation in community-based activities in smaller community-based services. Studies reporting improvements in community participation have reported increases in both the variety of community facilities used (e.g. Conneally et al, 1992) and the number of times community facilities are used (e.g. Bratt and Johnston, 1988; de Kock et al, 1988).

22

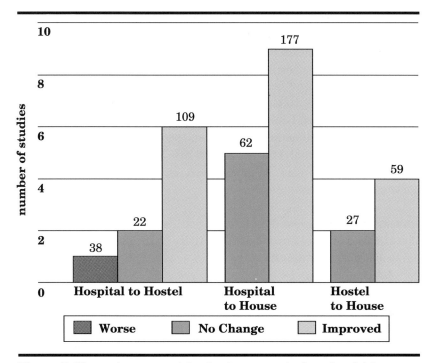

Figure 7: *Change in user participation in community-based activities across different types of services*

However, it should be noted that such improvements generally occur from a very low baseline in hospital settings, and that community contact in community-based services may still be relatively superficial and infrequent (Donegan and Potts, 1988; Fleming and Stenfert Kroese, 1990; Stanley and Roy, 1988), involving use of community facilities (e.g. walking in parks) that allow for little contact with ordinary members of the community (Lowe and de Paiva, 1991; Saxby et al, 1986). The frequency, variety and quality of community contacts may partly reflect the level of disabilities of service users. Thus, for example, Fleming and Stenfert Kroese (1990) report that people with more severe disabilities used a more restricted range of less demanding community facilities less frequently than users with less severe disabilities. Unfortunately, the majority of studies only examined the short-term effects of moving to less restrictive environments. The only study in the review which examined the use of community facilities over an extended, five year, period of time (Lowe and de Paiva, 1991), reported evidence of sustained increases in the use of community facilities by service users in small-scale staffed houses throughout the period of the study.

While it would appear (again rather unsurprisingly) that improvements in the use of community facilities are commonly associated with the move to smaller community-based residences, such increases are by no means inevitable.

Engagement

The direct observation of the extent to which users are actively engaged or participating in everyday on-going activities has been the most frequently used measure of outcome in UK research over the past 14 years (e.g. Auburn and Leach, 1989; Beail, 1988; Bratt and Johnston, 1988; Emerson et al, 1992, 1993; Felce et al, 1980, 1986a; Hemming et al, 1981; Mansell and Beasley, 1990; Mansell et al, 1984; Pettipher and Mansell, 1993; Rawlings, 1985a,b; Wood, 1989).

These observational studies record the activity of service users according to a number of pre-defined categories. *Engagement* is typically defined as either

- appropriate non-social activity (such as participation in leisure activity, personal care, domestic activity or an appropriate response to a formal programme) or

- social interaction between the user and others (usually staff and other service users).

Other codes commonly used in such studies include *neutral* activity (such as passivity, unpurposeful activity, aimless ambulation or smoking) and *inappropriate* service user behaviour (such as aggression to self, others or property or stereotyped behaviour). Studies typically evaluate the reliability of the observational method by having two observers simultaneously but independently code the activity of users for between 10 and 25% of the observation time.

This definition of engagement has been used with sufficient consistency across the studies to allow for the comparison of results across as well as within studies. Figure 8 presents such a comparison for all studies from which information relating to overall levels of user engagement was available. Each bar in the chart represents data pertaining to either the study as a whole or, where available, to each residential unit evaluated. It should be noted that the information in Figure 8 is based on studies rather than publications. This is important given the occasional occurrence of repeated presentations of the same data across multiple publications.

As can be seen, while levels of engagement were higher in staffed houses (average weighted for number of participants: 47.7%) than either community based hostels and hospital-based units (24.7%) or mental handicap hospitals (13.7%), significant variation occurred within each type of service. Thus, for example, engagement ranged from 2-23% in hospitals, 6-54% in hostels/units and 8-74% in staffed houses. To put these figures into perspective, they suggest that, over a 16 hour day, users in hospitals can expect to spend an average of 2 hours and 12 minutes (range 19 minutes to 3 hours 41 minutes) of their time actively participating in on-going activities. Over a similar period of time users in staffed houses can expect to spend an average of 7 hours 40 minutes (range 1 hour 17 minutes to 11 hours 50 minutes) of their time similarly engaged. Statistical analysis of these results indicated that, overall, type of service had a significant effect on level of engagement ($F=18.85$, $d.f.=55$, $p<0.0001$), due to levels of engagement in staffed houses being significantly higher than in either hospitals or hostels/units, which did not differ significantly from each other.

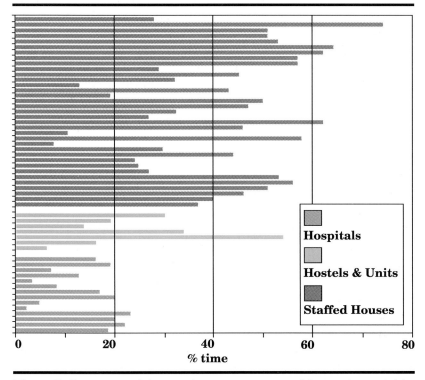

Figure 8: *Percentage of time service users are engaged in ongoing activities across studies and services*

Unfortunately, studies frequently failed to provide adequate descriptions of potentially significant characteristics of either the services (e.g. staffing ratios) or their users (e.g. levels of ability). This, when combined with the relatively small number of studies, precludes the use of statistical procedures to help identify those variables which may account for the observed variation within service models. However, Felce (1994) has reported that up to 82% of the variation in engagement data across individuals may be accounted for by two factors: the competence of service users and the amount of assistance (instructions, guidance, prompting) received from staff. Re-analysis of our own data (Emerson et al, 1993) indicates that up to 52% of variation within individuals over time in their level of engagement may be accounted for by the rate of assistance received by staff. Anecdotal evidence tends to suggest that those services in which high levels of staff assistance are provided are characterised not by the presence of additional staff resources, but by the implementation of a behaviourally-orientated model of providing 'whole environment' or 'active' support (Felce, 1988, 1991).

It is unlikely, however, that differences in the abilities of service users alone can account for the observed differences between types of service provision as similar results are obtained from longitudinal studies in which the same individuals are tracked over time as they move from hospital to community. Figure 9 presents a summary of within study differences for the 15 longitudinal and 11 comparison group studies which have directly compared levels of engagement in two or more types of services.

As can be seen, while the majority of comparisons (78%) indicate significantly increased levels of engagement in smaller community-based environments, a minority of studies, including 25% of comparisons between hospitals and community-based staffed housing reported no such significant change. We shall return to the issue of what predicts success in community-based provision in the final section of this report.

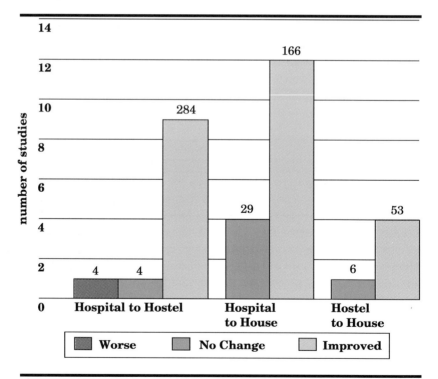

Figure 9: *Change in user engagement in ongoing activities across different types of services*

Status & Acceptance

Only four of the studies included in the review examined issues relating to the social status of service users in residential facilities, or their acceptance by members of local communities (Felce, 1989; Flynn, 1989; McConkey et al, 1993; Saxby et al, 1986). These studies interviewed either the neighbours of people with learning disabilities in community-based staffed houses (McConkey et al, 1993) or people managing and working in local businesses (e.g. shops, cafes) frequented by service users (Felce, 1989; Saxby et al, 1986) concerning their attitudes towards people with learning disabilities whom they met on a daily basis. Interviews with neighbours before and after people with learning disabilities had moved into neighbouring houses revealed that neighbours reported increased contact with people with learning disabilities and many fewer (and less serious) problems than they had initially anticipated. There was also a drop in neighbours' apparent willingness to help service users, although McConkey et al (1993) suggest that this was due largely to social desirability factors. Interviews with local business managers and assistants (Felce, 1989; Saxby et al, 1986) showed a large degree of acceptance of service users, with the majority of service users seen as not standing out to a large degree (except in noisiness), as presentable as the average customer and as showing reasonable behaviour. A majority also reported that having service users as customers was an advantage for the business, and almost all business managers and assistants reported that they thought service users benefited from living in the community. These positive findings can be contrasted with those of Flynn (1989), who found that a third of people with learning disabilities living independently reported victimization from non-disabled people in local communities.

This very small number of studies suggests that people without learning disabilities in local communities are relatively accepting of service users once day-to-day contact is achieved and sustained, although such acceptance is not inevitable. However, acceptance from people in local communities is not the same as meaningful involvement and participation in local communities (see above). It seems that, although a number of local people without learning disabilities may be willing to become more involved with service users, factors such as embarrassment may be a barrier to spontaneous meaningful interaction and involvement (McConkey et al, 1993).

Staff Contact

The extent and nature of contact received by users from care staff can be considered an intermediate outcome when evaluating the impact of the move from hospital to community. That is, while not clearly an outcome in itself (although contact with staff does constitute the main form of social contact received by people with learning disabilities in residential care), it may plausibly be related to the extent to which services achieve their aims.

Twenty-six studies included in the review examined the extent and nature of contact received by users from care staff, most frequently by employing some form of direct observation (e.g. Beail, 1989; Dalgleish and Matthews, 1980; Durward and Whatmore, 1976; Emerson et al, 1992; Felce et al, 1986a; Lowe et al, 1992; Orlowska et al, 1991; Thomas et al, 1986). The majority of these studies focused their observations on the activities of service users and consequently only observed those aspects of staff behaviour which involved active contact with users (e.g. Emerson et al, 1992, 1993). In such studies, staff contact was typically coded into the following categories, staff *assistance* (e.g. instructions or physical guidance to service users), *neutral* staff interaction with service users (e.g. chatting or holding a service user's hand), *positive* staff interaction with service users (e.g. praise, smiles or hugs) and *negative* staff interaction with service users (e.g. verbal disapproval or physical restraint). As with observational studies of user engagement, studies commonly evaluated the reliability of the data collected by having two observers simultaneously but independently code the activity of users for between 10 and 25% of the observation time.

These definitions and procedures to measure staff contact have been used with sufficient consistency to enable us to make comparisons of the results across as well as within studies. Figure 10 presents a comparison across all studies from which data relating to overall levels of staff contact was available. Each bar within the chart represents data pertaining to either the study as a whole or, where available, data pertaining to each residential unit evaluated. The percentages in Figure 10 are proportions of time in which the service user is receiving some form of staff contact, rather than proportions of staff time spent providing contact.

As can be seen, while overall levels of staff contact were higher in staffed houses (average weighted for the number of participants: 14.8%) than either hostels/units (9.3%) or NHS mental handicap hospitals (4.2%), again significant variation occurred within each type of service. Thus, for example, the amount of time users received contact from staff ranged from 3-16% in hospitals, 2-17% in hostels/units and 5-31% in community-based staffed houses. To put these figures into perspective they suggest that over a 16 hour day users in hospitals can expect to receive an average of 40 minutes (range 29 minutes to 2 hours 34 minutes) of contact from staff. Over a similar period of time users in staffed houses can expect to receive an average of 2 hours 22 minutes (range 48 minutes to 4 hours 58 minutes) of contact. While the small number of studies evaluating staff contact in hostels and units makes

28

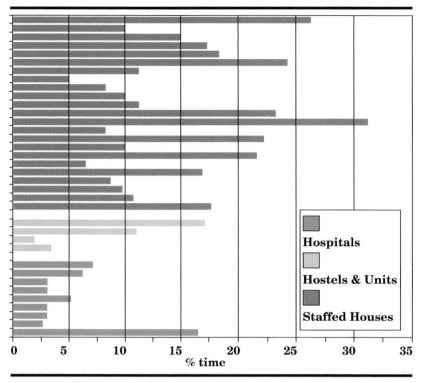

Figure 10: *Percentage of time service users receive staff contact across studies and services*

the assessment of the statistical significance of differences across all types of services impossible, a comparison of hospitals with staffed houses revealed that users in staffed houses received significantly more staff contact than users in hospitals (t=3.66, df=30, p<0.01).

Figure 11 presents a summary of within-study differences for those 16 studies which have directly compared levels of staff contact in two or more types of services.

As Figure 11 shows, while the majority of comparisons (79%) made within these studies reported significantly increased levels of staff contact in 'less restrictive' environments, a minority of studies, including 27% of comparisons between hospitals and community-based staffed housing reported no significant change.

While such variation both within and between service models is of considerable practical significance, relatively few studies reviewed here have explored possible determinants of staff contact and support to service users that might account for such variation. Other studies, however, have suggested that:

- only a tenuous relationship exists between the availability of resources (e.g. staff:user ratios) and the extent and nature of

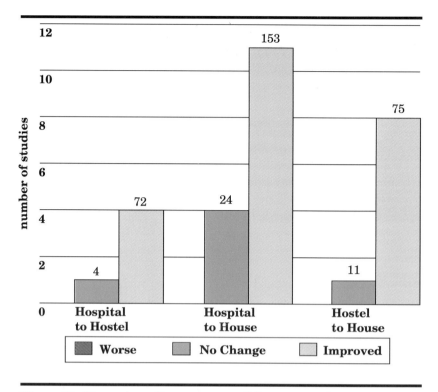

Figure 11: *Change in staff contact across different types of services*

staff:user interaction (e.g. Dalgleish and Matthews, 1981; Felce et al, 1991; Felce and Repp, 1992; Seys and Duker, 1988);

- increasing resources through staff training per se frequently fails to influence actual staff performance, although evidence does exist that practically-based approaches to training may result in some temporary improvements in performance (e.g. Reid et al, 1989; Ziarnik and Bernstein, 1982);

- the characteristics of service users (such as personal appearance and challenging behaviours) influence the quantity and quality of staff contact (e.g. Carr et al, 1991; Dailey et al, 1974; Emerson et al, 1992; Grant and Moores, 1977; Moores and Grant, 1977), although there is little evidence that positive changes in user behaviour act to increase or maintain staff contact (Woods and Cullen, 1983);

- while studies have generally found that staff contact in hospitals is relatively independent of service user behaviour (e.g. Beail, 1985; Felce et al, 1987), staff behaviour in community-based services has been found to be more contingent on service user behaviour (e.g. Felce et al, 1987), although the patterns of staff responses to the behaviour of users may in some cases act to sustain challenging behaviour (e.g. Hall and Oliver, 1992).

Outcomes for Carers and Care Staff

Six of the studies included in the review explored various aspects of outcomes for care staff supporting users in different types of services. These studies have focused either on

- parental attitudes and opinions concerning their son or daughter with learning disabilities living in residential services (Conneally et al, 1992; Emerson et al, 1993; Walker et al, 1993);

- aspects of staff stress, morale and staff turnover in services for people with learning disabilities (Dockrell et al, 1993; Emerson et al, 1993: Felce, 1989; Murphy et al, 1991; Walker et al, 1993).

Carers

Three of the studies included in the review explored parental opinions concerning the quality or appropriateness of the services provided for their daughter or son. All employed retrospective interviews with, or questionnaires completed by, parents, and generally reported a very high level of parental satisfaction with the community-based service provided (Conneally et al, 1992; Emerson et al, 1993; Walker et al, 1993). These findings, although encouraging, must be interpreted with some considerable caution, however, since studies in other countries (e.g. Conroy and Bradley, 1985; Tossebro, 1993) have found that parents with sons or daughters in institutional care also report themselves as being very satisfied with service provision, and are generally opposed to moves to community-based services, although these opinions change after their daughter or son has moved to a community-based service. These findings suggest a pervasive social desirability effect that has not been taken into account in the studies reviewed here.

Care Staff

The five studies examining outcomes for care staff have reported that:

- staff turnover rates vary between 10% to 25% per year in the UK with some evidence that turnover may be higher in community-based staffed housing services than in larger community units and institutions (Emerson et al, 1993; Felce, 1989);

- care staff report more optimism and job satisfaction but also higher levels of stress in smaller community-based settings than in institutions (Emerson et al, 1993; Murphy et al, 1991; see also Allen et al, 1990; Rose, 1993).

Although the reasons for such differences are undoubtedly complex, factors such as local economic conditions (Baumeister and Zaharia, 1986) and various features of care organisations (Hatton and Emerson, 1993) seem to be more important influences on staff stress and turnover than the service model per se. This suggests that much more attention needs to be paid to the structure and organisation of services for people with learning disabilities if staff stress and morale are to be improved, and staff turnover is to be contained (Hatton and Emerson, 1993).

Service Organisation

Twelve of the studies included in the review have examined various aspects of the service organisation and practices within services for people with learning disabilities. Most commonly, they have used a version of the Scale of Management Practices (King and Raynes, 1968; King et al, 1971; Pratt et al, 1979, 1980), designed to evaluate the extent to which practices within services resemble those of a total institution in the areas of: block treatment of service users; routines which act to depersonalise users; rigidity of routines; and maintaining a social distance between carers and users (e.g. Emerson et al, 1993; Hemming et al, 1981).

The results from these studies vary, with some studies reporting less restrictive management practices in smaller community-based settings than in hospitals (Hemming et al, 1981; Rawlings, 1985a,b), and others reporting either very limited change or no difference at all in management practices between settings (Beail, 1989; Emerson et al, 1993). From these studies, it appears that management practices in community-based services may often recreate those characterising total institutions (c.f. Sinson, 1990). This adds further weight to the argument that community-based services in themselves do not guarantee a high quality of life for service users, and combines with information concerning service user choice (see earlier) to suggest that in many important respects the life experience of service users in community-based services may not be radically different from that experienced in hospitals.

In addition to considering the extent to which services exhibit the characteristics of total institutions, studies have also examined service performance on purported indicators of service quality, such as the presence and detail of Individual Programme Plans (e.g. Hewson and Walker, 1992), and contact with health and welfare professionals (e.g. Bratt and Johnston, 1988). Information concerning Individual Programme Plans suggests that, while they may be more common in community-based services (Allen, 1990), they are not routinely implemented or maintained (Hewson and Walker, 1992). Studies concerning contact with health and welfare professionals suggests that such contact may decrease in the move from hospital to community settings (Bratt and Johnston, 1988; Emerson et al, 1993), although the implications of this for service quality are unclear.

Finally, a small number of studies have interviewed staff concerning their opinions of service organisation (e.g. Hewson and Walker, 1992; Walker et al, 1993). These studies have found that staff are generally unclear about service aims and service organisation (Hewson and Walker, 1992; Walker et al, 1993), with some staff reporting high levels of unmet service user need (Walker et al, 1993) and others reporting low levels of unmet service user need (Emerson et al, 1993).

The relatively small number of studies that have focused on service processes and service organisation provide a mixed picture of the quality of community services. While many community-based services show considerable improvement over hospitals in terms of the management practices used, this is not inevitable, and many services are reported to have poor service organisation, unclear service aims, and a lack of procedures for planning, implementing and monitoring programmes to enhance the quality of life of service users.

Costs

Eight of the studies included in the review contained information relating to the costs of different types of institutional and community-based services for people with learning disabilities in the UK (e.g. Davies, 1988; Emerson et al, 1993; Knapp et al, 1992; Shiell et al, 1992). While differences in the types of costs reported (e.g. capital costs, revenue costs or comprehensive costs) and differences in the methods used to calculate costs makes the comparison of costings data across studies impossible, many studies report within-study comparisons between service models.

- Studies reporting *capital costs* (e.g. Davies et al, 1991; Felce, 1981; Felce, 1989; Shiell et al, 1992) have generally found no association between capital costs per place and service setting, with places in staffed houses on average proving no more expensive than places in larger community-based units or hospitals.

- Studies reporting revenue costs (e.g. Davies, 1988; Felce, 1989; McGill et al, 1994) have generally found that revenue costs per service user are higher for community-based staffed houses than for larger community-based units or hospitals, although revenue costs in hospitals can rise dramatically as service users are resettled out of them (c.f. Korman and Glennerster, 1990).

- Studies reporting comprehensive costings (i.e. the cost of the entire service package provided to service users, including elements of capital and revenue costs) have reported wide variation in costs within service models (Emerson et al, 1993; Knapp et al, 1992; Shiell et al, 1992). Indeed, within-service variation is so large that no clear relationships emerge between type of service and comprehensive costings (Knapp et al, 1992; Shiell et al, 1992).

It seems that any relationship between service model and costs is likely to be complex, suggesting that economies of scale are likely to prove elusive. Although these studies provide useful information on service costs, they generally fail to explore the more contentious issue of the relationship between the quality and costs of services. Given the lack of consensus concerning how to measure either quality or costs, such limitations are perhaps not surprising, but a very small number of studies have attempted to address this issue. Generally, these studies report either a weak association (e.g. Cambridge et al, 1993; Shiell et al, 1993) or no association at all (e.g. Emerson et al, 1993) between service costs and indicators of service quality, pointing to the overriding importance of organisational factors (see earlier) for service quality and service user quality of life.

Issues and Conclusions

The research evidence which has accumulated since 1980 suggests that people with learning disabilities who move from larger scale institutional provision (primarily mental handicap hospitals) to smaller scale community-based services (primarily staffed houses) can, in general, expect:

- ✓ an *improvement in their material standard of living*;

- ✓ to be *more satisfied* with the services they receive and with their life in general;

- ✓ to have *more opportunities to use skills* which they possess as well as to *develop new competencies*;

- ✓ to spend *less time engaged in stereotypic behaviours* such as rocking;

- ✓ to have *more opportunities for choice* over routine daily activities;

- ✓ to have *more contacts with other people*;

- ✓ to make *more use of a greater variety of 'ordinary' community facilities*;

- ✓ to spend *more time engaged in constructive activities*;

- ✓ to be relatively *well accepted* by those who serve them in local businesses;

- ✓ to receive *more contact and support* from care staff;

- ✓ to be supported in a *less institutional* environment.

It is apparent, however, that these are far from inevitable consequences of the move to the community. On all measures of outcome the variation within community-based services was substantial. This suggests that for a significant minority of people life in 'the community' would appear to be relatively indistinguishable, on these measures of outcome at least, from life in hospital.

The same research also suggests that, compared to the general population, people who move to community-based services can also, in general, expect to:

× remain relatively *poor*;

× develop *few new skills* once they have settled in the community;

× to *continue to show more serious challenging behaviours*;

× to have *few, if any, opportunities for choice* over such life defining decisions as who to live with and who to be supported by;

× to have fewer opportunities to exercise *choice over everyday routine* matters than non-disabled people;

× to have *few relationships with non-disabled people*, other than care staff who are paid to be with them;

× to have *little real presence* in their communities;

× to *spend much of their day waiting* for activities to happen or to be engaged in passive and relatively purposeless activities;

× to receive little *contact* from staff.

This overview of the research evidence raises a number of important questions. What are the longer-term effects of the move to the community? What are the determinants of quality in community-based services? How successful are community-based services in enabling users to experience a quality of life commensurate with the rest of society? What is the way forward for providing residential care for people with learning disabilities?

Longer Term Effects

As we saw earlier, very few of the studies included in the review have investigated the longer-term effects of the move from hospital to community. Those that have addressed this issue have tended to indicate a levelling off in the rate of improvement in user competency following the immediate move to community-based residential provision (e.g. Lowe and de Paiva, 1991; Cambridge et al, 1993).

Two factors may account for this finding. Firstly, as we discussed earlier, evaluating change on the basis of information gained from care staff runs the risk that any changes may simply reflect changes in informant attitudes or expectations rather than actual changes in the behaviour, activities or lifestyle of service users. So, for example, differences in the expectations and experience of care staff employed in hospital and community settings may account, at least in part, for the reported increases in challenging behaviour and also help explain some positive outcomes, for example the reported developments in the competence of service users. If the reported changes do reflect differences in the expectations or experience of care staff then we should not be surprised to find that initial changes are maintained but not improved upon.

Alternatively, the reported pattern of change may reflect the increased opportunities available in community-based settings. So, for example, increased proximity in the community to shops, banks and leisure facilities is likely to overcome some transportation barriers to participation common in many institutional settings. Similarly, devolved budgeting and a reduction in the use of centralised purchasing and domestic services helps to create accessible opportunities for users to participate in a wider range of home-based activities.

Whatever the reason for this plateau effect over time, it is apparent that there is very little evidence that *within* community-based services users are developing new competencies, new relationships or extending the extent of their participation in their surrounding community over time.

The failure of the evaluation literature to take a longitudinal perspective when evaluating outcomes within community-based provision has also meant that very little is known regarding the continuity of care provided to users, an aspect of service performance which is often of major concern to informal carers. Thus, we know little about such issues as:

- the security of relationships between users and care staff;
- the chances of people being relocated within residential service systems (c.f. Altman and Cunningham, 1993);
- the probability that people will be excluded from community-based services;
- the factors underlying placement failure (c.f. Mansell et al, 1994);
- the fate of those people who are excluded.

While these omissions must be of concern to policy makers, purchasers and providers, it also illustrates the extent to which the research agenda has been dominated by the interests of researchers and their primary customers and may not reflect key concerns of carers or, indeed, the users of services.

The Determinants of Quality

The research which we have reviewed has focused on comparing aspects of quality *across* different types of services. As we have seen, it suggests that, while significant differences do exist between institutional and community-based provision, there are also substantial variations in the quality of community-based services themselves. So, for example, while users in staffed houses can expect to spend around seven and a half hours of a 16 hour day engaged in constructive activity (compared with just over two hours for users in hospital), this figure ranges between studies from just over one and a quarter to nearly twelve hours. As we discussed above, these differences cannot be solely accounted for by differences in the skill levels of service users.

Unfortunately, the same body of research has largely failed to address the question of what differentiates between the varying levels of quality observed *within* community-based services. To begin to answer this question we will need to look elsewhere. A review of the broader literature indicates that three factors may be important.

Firstly, the *human and financial resources* available within services are likely to be related to overall quality. Indeed, the injection of additional resources, either in terms of increasing staffing levels or the skills of care staff, is often regarded as a panacea for all service ills. Taking an objective look at the research literature, however, makes it readily apparent that the relationship between resources and quality is far from straightforward.

So, for example, although some of the studies we have reviewed report a weak overall association between quality and costs in residential services (e.g. Cambridge et al, 1993; Shiell et al, 1993), others have either failed to find any such association (e.g. Emerson et al, 1993) or have failed to identify any significant improvements in quality associated with the addition of significant levels of resources (e.g. Emerson et al, 1992). Similarly, the scant evidence which is available suggests that the size of residential settings has little effect on outcomes once service model and user ability have been taken into account. Thus, for example, some of the better outcomes associated with community-based services have been achieved in what, today, would be considered relatively large settings (e.g. Felce, 1989; Felce and Toogood, 1988). These findings are consistent with the much more extensive research evidence which points to the existence of a rather tenuous relationship between staff:user ratios, group size, training and the actual performance of care staff (Reid et al, 1989; Repp et al, 1987; Ziarnik and Bernstein, 1982). This evidence suggests that:

- the amount of contact received by users is largely unrelated to overall staff:user ratios (e.g. Felce et al, 1991; Hatton et al, 1994);

- although users being supported in small groups of 1 to 4 by one or two staff do receive more support (e.g. Felce et al, 1991);

- increasing the staff:user ratio in a setting does not necessarily lead to users receiving more support (e.g. Mansell et al, 1982; Seys and Duker, 1988);

- increasing staff skills and/or knowledge through training in itself rarely has any lasting impact on actual staff performance (e.g. Reid et al, 1989; Repp et al, 1987; Ziarnik and Bernstein, 1982).

This evidence does not, of course, deny the importance of human resources. Rather, it points to the reasonably obvious conclusion that an adequate level of resources may be a necessary but is certainly not a sufficient condition for providing high quality residential care.

If resources are a necessary but not sufficient condition for ensuring quality, this suggests that those aspects of the *internal organisation* of services which ensure the efficient and appropriate utilisation of resources are likely to play an important role in determining quality. On the basis of the demonstrated success of a number of pilot projects (Felce, 1989; Felce and Toogood, 1988; Felce et al, 1986a,b), including services for people with severely challenging behaviours (McGill et al, 1994; Emerson and McGill, 1993; Mansell and Beasley, 1993), Felce, Mansell and colleagues (Felce, 1988, 1989, 1991; Mansell et al, 1987, 1994; McGill and Toogood, 1994) have argued for the employment of an 'active support' model in community-based services for people with severe disabilities. McGill and Toogood (1994) describe this model as involving the use of clearly defined organisational procedures for determining:

- *what will happen* in terms of the types of activities, both routine and extraordinary, which a service user should be enabled to participate in;

- *when, where and with whom it will happen*;

- *how it will happen* in terms of the way in which an activity is done, and the extent and nature of the support and encouragement which the user will require to enable their participation; and

- *how it will be evaluated* in terms of judging the success of the service in improving the quality of life of the service user.

While there have been no controlled evaluations of the effect of introducing this model into services, four sources of evidence suggest that such an approach may be associated with better outcomes for service users. Firstly, as we saw earlier, the amount of active assistance given to service users is the one factor (apart from user ability) which is clearly associated with the extent to which users actively participate in on-going activities (Felce, 1994). Secondly, the approach was developed in pilot projects which have been shown to be associated with positive outcomes for service users (Felce, 1989; Felce and Toogood, 1988; Felce et al, 1986a,b; McGill et al, 1994; Emerson and McGill, 1993; Mansell and Beasley, 1993). Thirdly, failure of care staff to implement this approach within some of the pilot projects was associated with poorer outcomes for service users (McGill et al, 1994). Finally, there exists a substantial body of evidence suggesting that appropriate staff performance is dependent on the existence of clear structures to ensure that staff:

- have access to the necessary *resources*, including skills and knowledge;

- are given *clear expectations* about what they are required to do;

- receive effective and *appropriate feedback* which compares their *actual performance* against these expectations (Reid et al, 1989; Repp et al, 1988).

The above discussion highlights the importance for organisations of developing models or theories of the relationships between service inputs, processes and outcomes and of extending such 'theories of action' to areas of service performance which are less well understood. Indeed, it can be argued that the major impact of evaluative research in the fields of health and social care lie in the development of such models rather than in the technical demonstration of variations in outcomes across different approaches to service provision (c.f. Beyer and Trice, 1982; Bulmer, 1982).

While evidence may suggest that the 'active support' approach may be associated with better outcomes for service users, it is clear that such an approach is relatively rarely adopted in community-based services (e.g. Hughes and Mansell, 1990). In part, this would appear to be due to the (probably mistaken) view that the introduction of such a structured approach is in conflict with users' right to choose and the implementation of the concepts of normalisation and social role valorization (Emerson and McGill, 1989; McGill and Emerson, 1992). There is, of course, no inherent reason why providing a clear and efficient structure to guide the activities of care staff should diminish user choice. Indeed, it could be argued that formalising and making explicit the processes for choosing and scheduling activities and deciding on the nature of the support to be provided should create the conditions under which user control could be maximised.

The failure of services to implement or sustain models of 'good practice' highlights the importance of key *leadership and management*. These are likely to be particularly important in acquiring and sustaining sufficient resources, clarifying organisational policy and thus providing staff with clear performance expectations, supporting the establishment of appropriate internal structures within residential services and motivating staff to implement the procedures necessary to ensure quality lifestyles for people with learning disabilities. All of these tasks will, of course, be dependent upon the existence of effective information systems which provide the managing agency with useful data with regard to such issues as:

- the outcomes experienced by service users;

- the outcomes experienced by informal carers and paid staff;

- the implementation of procedures and processes which the organisation believes to be inextricably linked to achieving positive outcomes.

The importance of effective leadership in key roles is indicated by evidence of service decay over time (e.g. Blunden and Evans, 1988; Woods and Cullen, 1983) and the apparent reduction in quality associated with the more widespread implementation of the staffed housing model (Mansell, 1994). That is, while variation in user characteristics tends to mask the issue, there is an apparent trend for latter studies evaluating the move to staffed housing (e.g. Bratt and Johnston, 1988; Hughes and Mansell, 1990) to fail to report the degree of benefit associated with initial or subsequent pilot or demonstration studies (e.g. Felce et al, 1986a,b; Mansell and Beasley, 1993).

Unfortunately, the ability to exercise effective leadership in community-based services appears to be impeded by a lack of trained and experienced managers in this rapidly expanding field and some confusion over the notions of participative management and autonomous work groups. As Mansell and colleagues (1994) point out, dissatisfaction with hierarchical and bureaucratic management systems has led over recent years to an interest in the ideas of participative management, quality circles and autonomous work groups. They go on to warn, however, that such approaches are problematic when

"developed not so much in the spirit of 'we, the managers will support you moving in the directions we and you approve of' but of 'who knows what is supposed to happen in these services – so you can decide on your own'. Where staff are left to manage themselves they may become isolated and inward-looking and their norms and values may drift away from those of the wider community" (p.79).

Effective leadership and management is likely to prove even more important (and difficult) in dispersed services containing numerous semi-autonomous groups than in hospital provision.

These issues highlight the importance of organisational capability in determining performance and point to the corresponding need for future research to examine the longitudinal performance of residential service *systems*. The relative recency with which many community-based residential services have been established indicates that they may be experiencing some of the problems typically found in growing organisations. Thus, for example, they are likely to be in the process of shedding their reliance on informal networks and hopefully evolving into more bureaucratically efficient organisations. This analysis does suggest that the organisational capability of community-based service systems, in contrast with well established hospital systems, may be expected to increase over time. Clearly, in order to address this issue future research will need focus upon the performance of the service systems, rather than selected pilot projects, over time and to develop procedures for measuring organisational capability and linking these to outcomes for service users.

An Acceptable Quality of Life?

We have made the point on a number of occasions that the majority of studies included in the review have involved comparisons between services on a rather restricted range of outcome measures. While, at least more recently, this body of research has begun to incorporate indicators of the quality of life or lifestyle of service users (e.g. engagement, use of community-based facilities), some notable omissions continue to exist (cf. Emerson, 1985). In particular, very little attention has been paid to the measurement of:

- broad social indicators of an individual's material quality of life (e.g. wealth, disposable income, physical health, employment status);

- aspects of close personal or intimate relationships enjoyed by service users;

- opportunities for users to exercise choice or control over their lives;

- user's expressed satisfaction with the services they receive or their quality of life in general.

While the latter may, in part, reflect the severity of disability of some participants, such omissions are difficult to explain on the basis of technical difficulty or the resources required to collect such measures. A cynical interpretation of the causes of such omissions would perhaps suggest that evaluation research has focused on those aspects of quality of life on which change may be expected, whilst ignoring those aspects (e.g. poverty, user empowerment, close personal relationships) on which there exists a tacit understanding that 'care in the community' makes little difference.

We have also drawn attention to the fact that very few studies indeed have involved any normative judgements concerning the general adequacy, acceptability or decency of the quality of care provided or the quality of life experienced by people with learning disabilities (cf. Tossebro, 1993). Only one study in the current review incorporated comparisons between the lifestyle or quality of life of service users and non-disabled people (Stanley and Roy, 1988). While this study did report similar levels of life satisfaction and overall quality of life (but less use of community facilities) by adults with learning disabilities compared to a group of non-disabled adults in the local community, its reliance on care staff reports to judge the life satisfaction of users must be considered a serious flaw. Similarly, studies have failed to make comparison with other potentially significant reference groups, e.g. people with learning disabilities living with their families who have never been institutionalised.

As a result, while the existing body of research may point to the overall superiority of new smaller community-based services over previous hospital provision, it offers little information which may help to form a broader judgement regarding the adequacy, acceptability or decency of the quality of life experienced by people with learning disabilities in these new settings. That is, while community-based services provide a better quality of life for service users than mental handicap hospitals or medium sized units, is it good enough? How does it compare with the quality of life of non-disabled people?

Answering this question must surely form the basis of the research agenda for the coming decade. This is particularly important given the suggestion from the available evidence that the users of community-based residential services: are relatively poor; develop few new skills once they have settled in the community; have few, if any, opportunities for choice over such life defining decisions as who to live with and who to be supported by; have few opportunities to exercise choice over everyday routine matters; have few relationships with non-disabled people, other than care staff who are paid to be with them; have little real presence in their communities; spend much of their day waiting for activities to happen and receive little active support from staff.

The Way Forward

What are the conclusions which can be drawn from the research evidence relating to the move from hospital-based to 'community care'? Six general conclusions appear warranted.

- *People with learning disabilities, including those with more severe disabilities and additional needs such as sensory impairments or severely challenging behaviours can be supported in the community in such a way as to significantly improve their quality of life.*

- *Overall, smaller community-based residential services offer a better quality of life to users than either mental handicap hospitals or medium size hostels or 'community units'.*

- *Community-based services vary widely in terms of their quality, to the extent that, for a significant minority of individuals life in the community is little different from life in hospital.*

- *A structured 'active support' approach to organising the care environment appears to be associated with consistently better outcomes, at least for people with more severe disabilities. However, such an approach is relatively infrequently implemented in services.*

- *There is little evidence to suggest that within community-based services users are developing new competencies, new relationships or extending the extent of their participation in their surrounding community.*

- *While more needs to be known, it does appear that the quality of life offered in many community-based services falls far short of the values and ideals which underlay their development and may also fall short of common notions of decency or acceptability when applied to non-disabled people.*

Given that the movement to community-based services may be judged only a qualified success, where do we go from here? Do we seek to improve the quality of existing provision on the basis of the available evidence or are the models of community-based services which have developed in the UK fundamentally flawed?

As we have argued in the sections above, the apparent variations in quality *within* community-based residential services may, along with other evidence, give some guidance to those seeking to adopt an incremental or evolutionary approach to improving the quality of existing provision.

This would indicate that the **purchasers or commissioners** of residential services will need to develop their own capacity for effectively and efficiently measuring the outcomes associated with the services they are purchasing. They may also wish to ensure that these services possess the structural and procedural characteristics which the available evidence suggests are associated with positive outcomes. This would involve assessing whether services (among other things):

- have a clear and explicit orientation or mission to provide the support to enable a named person or persons with learning disabilities to live and participate in the community;
- exhibit the structural characteristics appropriate to community-based services in terms of size, location, design, internal appointments and staffing requirements;
- possess and implement clearly defined procedures for ensuring the participation of users in all aspects of the running of their home;
- have clearly defined and appropriate management arrangements with regard to such issues as devolved responsibility for catering, laundry, maintenance, recruitment, purchase of provisions and materials;
- consistently implement clearly defined procedures for selecting and scheduling activities and arranging for the support necessary to enable the service user(s) to participate fully in these activities;
- have clearly defined arrangements for service user(s) to access appropriate vocational, educational and leisure services;
- implement clearly defined and appropriate procedures for staff supervision;
- collect on a regular basis information concerning the quality of life experienced by the user(s) of the service.

Service **providers**, other than attending to the above requirements from purchasers, will need in particular to strengthen their capacity to effectively lead and manage dispersed semi-autonomous work groups. In addition, providers will need to pay greater attention to the development of systems for monitoring and safeguarding against the potential for abuse which exists in all types of service provision. The dispersed nature and increased visibility of community-based services present some particular challenges in this area.

In order to address some of the deficiencies noted within our review, **researchers** and those involved in local evaluations will need to:

- develop ways of involving users and carers in the identification of significant outcomes;

- establish the social validity (Schwartz and Baer, 1991), or the social significance, of the results arising from an evaluation project, in particular by assessing the quality of life experienced by people with learning disabilities against normative standards;

- begin to identify those individual and setting factors which may account for individual variation in people's response to the move from hospital to community;

- evaluate services on a broad range of outcomes in order to begin to identify whether different patterns of outcomes may be associated with different models of service provision;

- evaluate the outcomes associated with a broader range of approaches to residential care (e.g. supported living, village communities) in order to help ensure that more objective information is available to policy makers and those responsible for commissioning and purchasing services;

- evaluate the outcomes associated with different approaches to day services;

- attend to the development of models which seek to explain the links between service inputs, processes and outcomes;

- begin to address longer-term aspects of outcomes within community-based service systems.

Others have argued, however, that the models of residential provision which have emerged in the UK are fundamentally flawed (Kinsella, 1993a, b), a view consistent with broader analyses which typify 'community care' as an example of transinstitutionalisation (e.g. Scull, 1984). Such an approach indicates the need for the development of alternative approaches to service provision, as exemplified by, for example, the 'Supported Living' movement (Kinsella, 1993b).

What, in part, makes Supported Living distinctive is its central focus on the empowerment of people with learning disabilities and its radically individualistic model of action, in which the required performance of supporters or staff is seen as being primarily dependent on a deep personal commitment to the person with learning disabilities. This idea finds its expression in a proposed change of employment practices within services to emphasise the use of 'ordinary' people in life sharing arrangements. At present, however, no evidence is available regarding the types of outcomes for users which are associated with such arrangements.

One of the main lessons which may be derived from the history of human services is that a powerful rhetoric does not always translate into effective outcomes for service users (Scheerenberger, 1983; Scull, 1993; Wolfensberger, 1975). Let us hope that future research and evaluation will help cast light on the actual impact of alternative models of care and the future evolution of residential services for people with learning disabilities.

References

Allen, D. (1990). Evaluation of a community-based day service for people with profound mental handicaps and additional special needs. *Mental Handicap Research* **3**, 179-195.

Allen, P., Pahl, J. and Quine, L. (1990). *Care Staff in Transition*. HMSO: London.

Altman, B.M. and Cunningham, P.J. (1993). Dynamic process of movement in residential settings. *American Journal on Mental Retardation* **98**, 304-316.

Anninson, J.E. and Young, W.H.L. (1980). The future forms of residential services for mentally retarded people in Australia – a delphi study. *Australian and New Zealand Journal of Developmental Disabilities* **6**, 167-180.

Auburn, T.C. and Leach, S. (1989). An evaluation of the physical environment of two community based homes for the mentally handicapped. *The British Journal of Mental Subnormality,* **35**, 83-93.

Bank-Mikkelsen, N. (1980). Denmark. In *Normalisation, Social Integration and Community Services* (ed. R.J. Flynn and K.E. Nitsch). Pro-Ed: Austin, Texas.

Baumeister, A.A. and Zaharia, E.S. (1986). Withdrawal and commitment of basic-care staff in residential programs. In *Living Environments and Mental Retardation* (ed. S. Landesman, P.M. Vietze and M. J. Begab). AAMR: Washington DC.

Beail, N. (1985). The nature of interactions between nursing staff and profoundly multiply handicapped children. *Child: Care, Health and Development* **11**, 113-129.

Beail, N. (1988). A comparative observational study of the care provided at home for profoundly multiply handicapped children. *Behavioural Psychotherapy,* **16**, 285-296.

Beail, N. (1989). Evaluation of a staffed ordinary house for children with severe learning difficulties. *Child: Care, Health and Development* **15**, 117-127.

Beswick, J. (1992). Unpublished Ph.D. Thesis. University of Manchester: Manchester.

Beyer, J.M. and Trice, H.M. (1982). The utilization process: A conceptual framework and synthesis of empirical findings. *Administrative Science Quarterly* **27**, 591-622.

Blunden, R. and Allen, D. (1987). *Facing the Challenge: An ordinary life for people with learning difficulties and challenging behaviours*. King's Fund: London.

Blunden, R. and Evans, G. (1988). Long-term maintenance of staff and resident behaviour in a hospital ward for adults with mental handicaps: report of a six-year follow-up. *Mental Handicap Research* **1**, 115-126.

Booth, W., Booth, T. and Simons, K. (1990). Return journey: The relocation of adults from long-stay hospital into hostel accommodation. *British Journal of Mental Subnormality* **36**, 87-97.

Bratt, A. and Johnston, R. (1988). Changes in life style for young adults with profound handicaps following discharge from hospital care into a 'second generation' housing project. *Mental Handicap Research* **1**, 49-74.

Bruininks, R.H. and Lakin, K.C. (1985). *Living and Learning in the Least Restrictive Environment*. P.H. Brookes: Baltimore.

Bruininks, R.H., Meyers, C.E., Sigford, B.B. and Lakin, K.C. (1981). *Deinstitutionalization and Community Adjustment of Mentally Retarded People*. American Association on Mental Deficiency: Washington.

Bulmer, M. (1982). *The Uses of Social Research*. Allen and Unwin: London.

Butler, E.W. and Bjaanes, A.T. (1983). Deinstitutionalization, environmental normalization and client normalization. In *Environments and Behavior* (eds. K.T. Kernan, M.J. Begab and R.B. Edgerton). University Park Press: Baltimore.

Cambridge, P., Hayes, L. and Knapp, M. (1993). *Care in the Community: Five Years On*. PSSRU: Kent.

Carr, E.G., Taylor, J.C. and Robinson, S. (1991). The effects of severe behavior problems in children on the teaching behavior of adults. *Journal of Applied Behavior Analysis* **24**, 523-535.

Cattermole, M., Jahoda, A. and Markova, I. (1988). Leaving home: the experience of people with a mental handicap. *Journal of Mental Deficiency Research* **32**, 47-57.

Clare, I.C.H. and Murphy, G.H. (1993). M.I.E.T.S. (Mental Impairment Evaluation & Treatment Service): A service option for people with mild mental handicaps & challenging behaviour &/or psychiatric problems. *Mental Handicap Research* **6**, 70-91.

Conneally, S., Boyle, G. and Smyth, F. (1992). An evaluation of the use of small group homes for adults with a severe and profound mental handicap. *Mental Handicap Research* **5**, 146-168.

Conroy, J. (1980). *Reliability of the Behavior Development Survey* (Tech. Rep. No. 80-1-1). Temple University Developmental Disabilities Center: Philadelphia.

Conroy, J.W. and Bradley, V.J. (1985). *The Pennhurst Longitudinal Study: A Report of 5 Years of Research and Analysis*. Human Services Research Institute: Boston.

Cragg, R. and Harrison, J. (1984). *Living in a Supervised Home: A Questionnaire of Quality of Life* (pilot version). West Mids Campaign for People with Mental Handicaps: Birmingham.

Cullen, C., Whoriskey, M., Mackenzie, K., Mitchell, W., Ralston, K., Shreeve, S. and Stanley, A. (in press). The effects of deinstitutionalization for adults with mental retardation. To appear in *Journal of Intellectual Disability Research*.

Dailey, W.F., Allen, G.J., Chinsky, J.M. and Veit, S.W. (1974). Attendant behavior and attitudes toward institutionalised retarded children. *American Journal of Mental Deficiency* **78**, 586-591.

Dalgleish, M. and Matthews, R. (1980). Some effects of environmental design on the quality of day care for severely mentally handicapped adults. *British Journal of Mental Subnormality,* **26**, 94-102.

Dalgleish, M. and Matthews, R. (1981). Some effects of staffing levels and group size on the quality of day care for severely mentally handicapped adults. *British Journal of Mental Subnormality,* **27**, 30-35.

Davies, L. (1988). Community care: the costs and quality. *Health Services Management Research* **1**, 145-155.

Davies, L., Felce, D., Lowe, K. and de Paiva, S. (1991). The evaluation of NIMROD, a community-based service for people with mental handicap: revenue costs. *Health Services Management Research* **4**, 170-180.

de Kock, U., Saxby, H., Thomas, M. and Felce, D. (1988). Community and family contact: An evaluation of small community homes for adults with severe and profound mental handicaps. *Mental Handicap Research* **1**, 127-140.

Department of Health (1989). *Needs and Responses*. Department of Health Leaflets Unit: Stanmore.

Department of Health (1993). *Services for People with Learning Disabilities and Challenging Behaviour or Mental Health Needs*. HMSO: London.

Department of Health and Social Security (1984). *Helping Mentally Handicapped People with Special Problems*. HMSO: London.

Dockrell, J., Gaskell, G., Rehman. H. and Normand, C. (1993). Service provision for people with mild learning difficulty and challenging behaviours: The MIETS evaluation. In *Research To Practice?* (ed. C. Kiernan). BILD: Clevedon.

Doll, E.A. (1953). *The Measurement of Social Competence: A Manual for the Vineland Social Maturity Scale*. Educational Test Bureau: Washington.

Durward, L. and Whatmore, R. (1976). Testing measures of the quality of residential care: a pilot study. *Behaviour Research and Therapy*, **14**, 149-157.

Emerson, E. (1985). Evaluating the impact of deinstitutionalization on the lives of mentally retarded people. *American Journal of Mental Deficiency* **90**, 277-288.

Emerson, E. (1990). Designing individualised community based placements as alternatives to institutions for people with a severe mental handicap and severe problem behaviour. In *Key Issues in Mental Retardation Research* (ed. W. Fraser). Routledge: London.

Emerson, E. (1992). What is normalisation?. In *Normalisation: A Reader for the 1990's* (ed. H. Smith and H. Brown). Routledge: London.

Emerson, E. and McGill, P. (1989). Normalisation and applied behaviour analysis: Values and technology in services for people with learning difficulties. *Behavioural Psychotherapy* **17**, 101-117.

Emerson, E. and McGill, P. (1993). Developing services for people with severe learning disabilities and seriously challenging behaviours: South East Thames Regional Health Authority, 1985-1991. In *People with Learning Disability and Severe Challenging Behaviour: New Developments in Services and Therapy* (ed. I. Fleming and B. Stenfert Kroese). Manchester University Press: Manchester.

Emerson, E., Beasley, F., Offord, G. and Mansell, J. (1992). Specialised housing for people with seriously challenging behaviours. *Journal of Mental Deficiency Research* **36**, 291-307.

Emerson, E., Cooper, J., Hatton, C., Beecham, J., Hallam, A., Knapp, M. and Cambridge, P. (1993). *An Evaluation of the Quality and Costs of Residential Further Education Services Provided by SENSE-Midlands*. Hester Adrian Research Centre: Manchester.

Evans, G., Todd, S., Blunden, R., Porterfield, J. and Ager, A. (1985). *A New Style of Life: The Impact of Moving into an Ordinary House on the Lives of People with a Mental Handicap*. Mental Handicap in Wales – Applied Research Unit: Cardiff.

Felce, D. (1981). The capital costs of alternative residential facilities for mentally handicapped people. *British Journal of Psychiatry* **139**, 230-237.

Felce, D. (1988). Behavioral and social climate in community group residences. *In Community Residences for Persons with Developmental Disabilities* (ed. M. Janicki, M.W. Krauss and M.M. Seltzer). P.H. Brookes: Baltimore.

Felce, D. (1989). *The Andover Project: Staffed Housing for Adults with Severe or Profound Mental Handicaps*. British Institute on Mental Handicap: Kidderminister.

Felce, D. (1991). Using behavioural principles in the development of effective housing services for adults with severe or profound handicap. In *The Challenge of Severe Mental Handicap: A Behaviour Analytic Approach* (ed. B. Remington). Wiley: Chichester.

Felce, D. (1994). The quality of support for ordinary living: staff:resident interactions and resident activity. In *The Dissolution of Institutions: An International Perspective* (ed. J. Mansell and K. Ericcson). Chapman and Hall: London.

Felce, D. and Perry, J. (in press). Quality of life: A contribution to its definition and measurement. To appear in Research in Developmental Disabilities.

Felce, D. and Repp, A. (1992). The behavioral and social ecology of community houses. *Research in Developmental Disabilities,* **13**, 27-42.

Felce, D. and Toogood, S. (1988). *Close to Home*. BIMH: Kidderminster.

Felce, D., Kushlick, A. and Mansell, J. (1980). Evaluation of alternative residential facilities for the severely mentally handicapped in Wessex: staff recruitment and continuity. *Advances in Behaviour Research and Therapy* **3**, 31-35.

Felce, D., Kushlick, A. and Mansell, J. (1980). Evaluation of alternative residential facilities for the severely mentally handicapped in Wessex: client engagement. *Advances in Behaviour Research and Therapy* **3**, 13-18.

Felce, D., Lowe, K. and de Paiva, S. (1994). Ordinary housing for people with severe learning disabilities and challenging behaviours. In *Severe Learning Disabilities and Challenging Behaviours: Designing High Quality Services*, (ed. E. Emerson, P. McGill and J. Mansell). Chapman and Hall: London.

Felce, D., Mansell, J. and Kushlick, A. (1980). Evaluation of alternative residential facilities for the severely mentally handicapped in Wessex: Revenue costs. *Advances in Behaviour Research and Therapy* **3**, 43-47.

Felce, D., Mansell, J. and Kushlick, A. (1980). Evaluation of alternative residential facilities for the severely mentally handicapped in Wessex: staff performance. *Advances in Behaviour Research and Therapy* **3**, 25-30.

Felce, D., Repp, A., Thomas, M., Ager, A. and Blunden, R. (1991). The relationship of staff:client ratios, interactions, and residential placement. *Research in Developmental Disabilities* **12**, 315-331.

Felce, D., Saxby, H., de Kock, U., Repp, A., Ager, A. and Blunden, R. (1987). To what behaviors do attending adults respond? A replication. *American Journal of Mental Deficiency* **91**, 496-504.

Felce, D., Thomas, M., de Kock, U., Saxby, H. and Repp, A. (1985). An ecological comparison of small community based houses and traditional institutions: Physical setting and the use of opportunities. *Behaviour Research and Therapy* **23**, 337-348.

Felce, D., de Kock, U. and Repp, A. (1986). An eco-behavioral analysis of small community based houses and traditional large hospitals for severely and profoundly mentally handicapped adults. *Applied Research in Mental Retardation* **7**, 393-408.

Felce, D., de Kock, U., Thomas, M. and Saxby, H. (1986). Change in adaptive behaviour of severely and profoundly mentally handicapped adults in different residential settings. *British Journal of Psychology,* **77**, 489-501.

Fleming, I. and Stenfert Kroese, B. (1990). Evaluation of a community care project for people with learning difficulties. *Journal of Mental Deficiency Research* **34**, 451-464.

Flynn, M. (1989). *Independent Living for Adults with Mental Handicap: 'A Place of My Own'.* Cassell Educational: London.

Grant, G.W. and Moores, B. (1977). Resident characteristics and staff behavior in two hospitals for mentally retarded adults. *American Journal of Mental Deficiency* **82**, 259-265.

Greig, R. (1993). The replacement of hospital services with community services based on individual need, Hester Adrian Research Centre Conference on Hospital Closure.

Gunzburg, H.C. (1968). *Social Competence and Mental Handicap.* Baillere, Tindall & Cassell: London.

Gunzburg, H.C. (1974). *The PAC Manual*, 3rd Edition. NSMHC: London.

Guy's Health District (1981). *Development Group for Services for Mentally Handicapped People: Report to the District Management Team.* Guy's Health District: London.

Hall, S. and Oliver, C. (1992). Differential effects of severe self-injurious behaviour on the behaviour of others. *Behavioural Psychotherapy* **20**, 355-365.

Haney, J.I. (1988). Empirical support for deinstitutionalization. In *Integration of Developmentally Disabled Individuals into the Community* (eds. L.W. Heal, J.I. Haney and A.R. Novak Amado). Paul H. Brookes: Baltimore.

Hatton, C. and Emerson, E. (1993). Organizational predictors of staff stress, satisfaction, and intended turnover in a service for people with multiple disabilities. *Mental Retardation* **31**, 388-395.

Hatton, C., Emerson, E., Robertson, J., Henderson, D. and Cooper, J. (1994). *An Evaluation of the Quality and Costs of Services for Adults with Severe Learning Disabilities and Sensory Impairments.* Hester Adrian Research Centre: Manchester.

Hemming, H. (1986). Follow-up of adults with mental retardation transferred from large institutions to new small units. *Mental Retardation* **24**, 229-235.

Hemming, H., Lavender, T. and Pill, R. (1981). Quality of life of mentally retarded adults transferred from large institutions to new small units. *American Journal of Mental Deficiency* **86**, 157-169.

Hewson, S. and Walker, J. (1992). The use of evaluation in the development of a staffed residential service for adults with mental handicap. *Mental Handicap Research* **5**, 188-203.

Hoefkens, A. and Allen, D. (1990). Evaluation of a special behaviour unit for people with mental handicaps and challenging behaviour. *Journal of Mental Deficiency Research* **34**, 213-228.

Holmes, N., Shah, A. and Wing, L. (1982). The disability assessment schedule: A brief screening device for use with the mentally retarded. *Psychological Medicine* **12**, 879-890.

Horner, R.D. (1980). The effects of an environmental 'enrichment' program on the behavior of institutionalized profoundly retarded children. *Journal of Applied Behavior Analysis* **13**, 473-491.

Hughes, H. and Mansell, J. (1990). *Consultation to Camberwell Health Authority Learning Difficulties Care Group: Evaluation Report.* CAPSC, University of Kent at Canterbury: Canterbury.

Jacobsen, J.W. and Schwartz, A.A. (1991). Evaluating living situations of people with developmental disabilities. In *Handbook of Mental Retardation* (eds. J.L. Matson and J.A. Mulick). Pergamon: New York.

Jahoda, A., Cattermole, M. and Markova, I. (1990). Moving out: an opportunity for friendship and broadening social horizons? *Journal of Mental Deficiency Research* **34**, 127-139.

Janicki, M., Krauss, M.W. and Seltzer, M.M. (1988). *Community Residences for Persons with Developmental Disabilities.* P.H. Brookes: Baltimore.

Jeffree, D. and Cheseldine, S. (1982). *Pathways To Independence: Checklists of Self-Help, Personal and Social Skills.* Hodder and Stoughton: Sevenoaks.

Joyce, T., Mansell, J. and Gray, H. (1989). Evaluating service quality: A comparison of diaries with direct observation. *Mental Handicap Research* **2**, 38-46.

King's Fund (1980). *An Ordinary Life: Comprehensive locally-based residential services for mentally handicapped people.* King's Fund Centre: London.

King's Fund (1984). *An Ordinary Working Life: Vocational services for people with mental handicap.* King's Fund Centre: London.

King's Fund (1989). *An Ordinary Life and Treatment Under Security for People with Mental Handicap.* King's Fund Centre: London.

Kinsella, P. (1993a). *Group Homes.* National Development Team: Manchester.

Kinsella, P. (1993b). *Supported Living: A New Paradigm*. National Development Team: Manchester.

Knapp, M., Cambridge, P., Thomason, C., Beecham, J., Allen, C. and Darton, R. (1992). *Care in the Community: Challenge and Demonstration*. Ashgate: Aldershot.

Korman, N. and Glennerster, H. (1990). *Hospital Closure*. Open University Press: Milton Keynes.

Locker, D., Rao, B. and Weddell, J.M. (1984). Evaluating community care for the mentally handicapped adult: a comparison of hostel, home and hospital care. *Journal of Mental Deficiency Research,* **28**, 189-198.

Lowe, K. and de Paiva, S. (1990). *The Evaluation of NIMROD, a community based service for people with mental handicap.* Mental Handicap in Wales – Applied Research Unit: Cardiff.

Lowe, K. and de Paiva, S. (1991). *NIMROD: An Overview.* HMSO: London.

Lowe, K., Beyer, S., Kilsby, M. and Felce, D. (1992). Activities and engagement in day services for people with a mental handicap. *Journal of Intellectual Disability Research,* **36**, 489-503.

Lowe, K., de Paiva, S. and Felce, D. (1993). Effects of a community-based service on adaptive and maladaptive behaviours: a longitudinal study. *Journal of Intellectual Disability Research* **37**, 3-22.

Malin, N.A. (1982). Group homes for mentally handicapped adults: residents' views on contact and support. *British Journal of Mental Subnormality* **28**, 29-34.

Malin, N. (1987). *Reassessing Community Care*. Croom Helm: Beckenham.

Mansell, J. (1994). Management issues in community services in Britain. In *The Dissolution of Institutions: An International Perspective* (ed. J. Mansell and K. Ericcson). Chapman and Hall: London.

Mansell, J. and Beasley, F. (1990). Evaluating the transfer to community care. In *Key Issues in Mental Retardation Research* (ed. W. Fraser). Routledge: London.

Mansell, J. and Beasley, F. (1993). Small staffed houses for people with severe learning disabilities and challenging behaviours. *British Journal of Social Work* **23**, 329-344.

Mansell, J., Felce, D., Jenkins, J. and de Kock, U. (1982). Increasing staff ratios in an activity with severely mentally handicapped people. *British Journal of Mental Subnormality* **28**, 97-99.

Mansell, J., Felce, D., Jenkins, J., de Kock, U. and Toogood, S. (1987). *Developing Staffed Housing for People with Mental Handicaps*. Costello: Tunbridge Wells.

Mansell, J., Hughes, H. and McGill, P. (1994). Maintaining local residential placements. In *Severe Learning Disabilities and Challenging Behaviours: Designing High Quality Services* (ed. E. Emerson, P. McGill and J. Mansell). Chapman & Hall: London.

Mansell, J., Jenkins, J., Felce, D. and de Kock, U. (1984). Measuring the activity of severely and profoundly mentally-handicapped adults in ordinary housing. *Behaviour Research and Therapy,* **22**, 23-29.

McConkey, R., Walsh, P.N. and Conneally, S. (1993). Neighbours' reactions to community services: contrasts before and after services open in their locality. *Mental Handicap Research* **6**, 131-141.

McGill, P. and Emerson, E. (1992). Behaviourism and social role valorization. In *Normalisation: A Reader for the 1990's* (eds. H. Smith and H. Brown). London: Routledge.

McGill, P. and Toogood, S. (1993). Organising community placements. In *Severe Learning Disabilities and Challenging Behaviours: Designing High Quality Services* (eds. E. Emerson, P. McGill and J. Mansell). Chapman & Hall: London.

McGill, P., Emerson, E. and Mansell, J. (1994). Individually designed residential provision for people with seriously challenging behaviours. In *Severe Learning Disabilities and Challenging Behaviours: Designing High Quality Services* (eds. E. Emerson, P. McGill and J. Mansell). Chapman and Hall: London.

McHatton, M., Collins, G. and Brooks, E. (1988). Evaluation in practice: moving from a 'problem' ward to a staffed flat. *Mental Handicap Research* **1**, 141-151.

Markova, I., Jahoda, A., Cattermole, M. and Woodward, D. (1992). Living in hospital and hostel: the pattern of interactions of people with learning difficulties. *Journal of Intellectual Disability Research,* **36**, 115-127.

Martindale, A. and Kilby, C.A. (1982). Closure of an old mental handicap hospital and the short-term and long-term effects on residents. *The British Journal of Mental Subnormality,* **28**, 3-12.

Moores, B. and Grant, G.W. (1977). The 'avoidance' syndrome in hospitals for the mentally handicapped. *International Journal of Nursing Studies* **14**, 91-95.

Murphy, G. and Clare, I. (1991). MIETS: a service option for people with mild mental handicaps & challenging behaviour or psychiatric problems: 2 assessment treatment & outcome for service users & service effectiveness. *Mental Handicap Research* **4**, 180-206.

Murphy, G. (1994). Understanding challenging behaviour. In *Severe Learning Disabilities and Challenging Behaviours: Designing High Quality Services* (ed. E. Emerson, P. McGill and J. Mansell). Chapman and Hall: London.

Murphy, G., Holland, A., Fowler, P. and Reep, J. (1991). MIETS: a service option for people with mild mental handicaps and challenging behaviour or psychiatric problems. *Mental Handicap Research* **4**, 41-66.

Nihira, K., Foster, R., Schellhaas, N. and Leland, H. (1974). *AAMD Adaptive Behavior Scale: Manual*. Pro-ED: Austin, TX.

Nirje, B. (1992). *The Normalization Principle Papers*. Centre for Handicap Research: Uppsala, Sweden.

Nisbet, J., Clark, M. and Covert, S. (1991). Living it up! An analysis of research on community living. In *Critical Issues in the Lives of People with Severe Disabilities* (eds. L.H. Meyer, C.A. Peck and L. Brown). Paul H. Brookes: Baltimore.

North Western Regional Health Authority (1983). *A Model District Service*. NWRHA: Manchester.

O'Brien, J. (1987). A guide to life style planning: Using The Activities Catalogue to integrate services and natural support systems. In *The Activities Catalogue: An Alternative Curriculum for Youth and Adults with Severe Disabilities* (ed. B.W. Wilcox and G.T. Bellamy). Brookes: Baltimore.

O'Brien, J. (1994). Down stairs that are never your own: Supporting people with developmental disabilities in their own homes. *Mental Retardation* **32**, 1-6.

O'Brien, J. and Tyne, A. (1981). *The Principle of Normalisation: A Foundation for Effective Services*. The Campaign for Mentally Handicapped People: London.

Orlowska, D., McGill, P. and Mansell, J. (1991). Staff-staff and staff-resident verbal interactions in a community-based group home for people with moderate and severe mental handicaps. *Mental Handicap Research* **4**, 3-19.

Parmenter, T. (1992). Quality of life of people with developmental disabilities. In *International Review of Research in Mental Retardation*, 18 (ed. N.W. Bray). Academic Press: New York.

Pettipher, C. and Mansell, J. (1993). Engagement in meaningful activity in day centres: an exploratory study. *Mental Handicap Research,* **6**, 263-274.

Pratt, M.W., Luszcz, M.A. and Brown, M.E. (1979). *Indices of Care in Small Community Residences*. Psychology Department, Mount St Vincent University: Halifax, Nova Scotia.

Pratt, M.W., Luszcz, M.A. and Brown, M.E. (1980). Measuring the dimensions of the quality of care in small community residences. *American Journal of Mental Deficiency* **85**, 188-194.

Rawlings, S. (1985a). Behaviour and skills of severely retarded adults in hospitals and small residential homes. *British Journal of Psychiatry* **146**, 358-366.

Rawlings, S. (1985b). Life-styles of severely retarded non-communicating adults in hospitals and small residential homes. *British Journal of Social Work,* **15**, 281-293.

Reid, D.H., Parsons, M.B. and Green, C.W. (1989). *Staff Management in Human Services: Behavioral Research and Application.* Charles C. Thomas: Springfield, Ill.

Repp, A.C., Felce, D. and de Kock, U. (1987). Observational studies of staff working with mentally retarded persons: A review. *Research in Developmental Disabilities* **8**, 331-350.

Repp, A.C., Felce, D. and Barton, L.E. (1988). Basing the treatment of stereotypic and self-injurious behaviors on hypotheses of their causes. *Journal of Applied Behavior Analysis* **21**, 281-289.

Rose, J. (1993). Stress and staff in residential settings: The move from hospital to the community. *Mental Handicap Research* **6**, 312-332.

Saxby, H., Thomas, M., Felce, D. and de Kock, U. (1986). The use of shops, cafes and public houses by severely and profoundly mentally handicapped adults. *British Journal of Mental Subnormality* **32**, 69-81.

Scheerenberger, R.C. (1983). *A History of Mental Retardation.* P.H. Brookes: Baltimore.

Schalock, R.L. (1990). *Quality of Life: Perspectives and Issues.* American Association on Mental Retardation: Washington, DC.

Schwartz, I.S. and Baer, D.M. (1991). Social validity assessments: Is current practice state of the art? *Journal of Applied Behavior Analysis* **24**, 189-204.

Scull, A.T. (1984). *Decarceration: Community Treatment of the Deviant – A Radical View* (2nd. Edition). Polity Press: Cambridge.

Scull, A.T. (1993). *The Most Solitary of Afflictions: Madness and Society in Britain, 1700-1900.* Yale University Press: New Haven.

Segal, S.S. (1990). *The Place of Special Villages & Residential Communities.* A.B. Academic Publishers: London.

Seys, D. and Duker, P. (1988). Effects of staff management on the quality of residential care for mentally retarded individuals. *American Journal on Mental Retardation* **93**, 290-299.

Shiell, A., Pettipher, C., Raynes, N. and Wright, K. (1992). The costs of community residential facilities for adults with a mental handicap in England. *Mental Handicap Research* **5**, 115-129.

Shiell, A., Pettipher, C., Raynes, N. and Wright, K. (1993). A cost-function analysis of residential services for adults with a learning disability. *Health Economics* **2**, 247-256.

Simon, G.B. (1981). *Local Services for Mentally Handicapped People.* British Institute of Mental Handicap: Kidderminster.

Sinson, J.C. (1990). Micro-institutionalisation? Environmental and managerial influences in ten living units for people with mental handicap. *British Journal of Mental Subnormality* **36**, 77-86.

Sparrow, S.S., Balla, D.A. and Cicchetti, D.V. (1984). *Vineland Adaptive Behavior Scale.* American Guidance Service: Circle Pines, MN.

Stanley, B. and Roy, A. (1988). Evaluating the quality of life of people with mental handicaps: A social validation study. *Mental Handicap Research* **1**, 197-210.

Thomas, M., Felce, D., de Kock, U., Saxby, H. and Repp, A. (1986). The activity of staff and of severely and profoundly mentally handicapped adults in residential settings of different sizes. *British Journal of Mental Subnormality,* **32**, 82-92.

Toogood, R.J. (1974). *Calculating Nursing Needs.* Apex 1, 17-18.

Tossebro, J. (1993). Background and prospects of institutional closure in Norway, Hester Adrian Research Centre Conference on Hospital Closure.

Towell, D. (1988). *An Ordinary Life in Practice.* King's Fund: London.

Towell, D. and Beardshaw, V. (1991). *Enabling Community Integration.* King's Fund: London.

Walker, C., Ryan, T. and Walker, A. (1993). *Quality of Life After Resettlement for People with Learning Disabilities. Summary of the Report to the North West Regional Health Authority.* Department of Sociological Studies: Sheffield.

Williams, C. (1986). *The Social Training Achievement Record (STAR) Profile* (2nd ed.). BIMH Publications: Kidderminster.

Wing, L. and Gould, J. (1979). Systematic recording of behaviours and skills of retarded and psychotic children. *Journal of Autism and Childhood Schizophrenia* **8**, 79-97.

Wing, L., Holmes, N. and Shah, A. (1985). *Residents' Opinions and Behaviour Schedule* (Darenth Park). Institute of Psychiatry: London.

Wolfensberger, W. (1975). *The Origin and Nature of Our Institutional Models.* Human Policy Press: Syracuse.

Wolfensberger, W. (1992). *A Brief Introduction to Social Role Valorization as a High-Order Concept for Structuring Human Services.* Syracuse University: Syracuse NY.

Wood, J. (1989). Comparing interactions in two hospital wards for people with mental handicaps: a pilot study. *Mental Handicap Research,* **2**, 3-17.

Woods, P. and Cullen, C. (1983). Determinants of staff behaviour in long-term care. *Behavioural Psychotherapy* **11**, 4-17.

Ziarnik, J.P. and Bernstein, G.S. (1982). A critical examination of the effect of inservice training on staff performance. *Mental Retardation* **20**, 109-114.

Appendix – Studies Reviewed

Study	Settings	Design	Numbers	Domains Measured	Summary of Results
Allen (1990)	1) Special Care Unit Day Service 2) Community Day Service	Comparison groups	1) 11 adults 2) 11 adults	Lifestyle: engagement Lifestyle: presence Lifestyle: participation Lifestyle: social status Service processes	Community Day Service: greater engagement, less neutral, inappropriate activities; more activities in integrated settings; greater number and variety of activities; activities rated as more age-appropriate and desirable; more IPPs, more emphasis on community experiences, less emphasis on self-help skills.
Auburn & Leach (1989)	1) Community Staffed House A 2) Community Staffed House B	Comparison groups	1) 18 adults 2) 8 adults	Lifestyle: participation	Home B: less time in bedrooms, less social interaction, more leisure activities.
Beail (1985)	1) Mental Handicap Hospital	n/a	1) 10 children	Lifestyle: engagement Staff contact	Children spend most of time doing neutral or no behaviours; Very low level of staff contact, more positive than negative contact, positive contact not contingent on appropriate child behaviour.
Beail (1988)	1) Mental Handicap Hospital 2) Family Home	Comparison groups	1) 4 children 2) 4 children	Lifestyle: engagement Staff contact	Family Home: more engagement, less inappropriate or neutral activity; more responses from carers, carer responses more contingent on child behaviour.

Study	Settings	Design	Numbers	Domains Measured	Summary of Results
Beail (1989)	1) Community Residential Unit	n/a	1) 6 children	Lifestyle: engagement Service processes Staff contact	Mean 44% appropriate, 25% inappropriate, 31% neutral behaviour; similar level of institutional practices to hospital wards in other studies; staff responses contingent on child behaviour.
Beswick (1992)	1) Mental Handicap Hospital 2) Variety of Community Settings, largely Staffed Houses	Mixed Design: a) Longitudinal (post-move data collected at 6 time points); b) Comparison group 'Movers' vs. 'Stayers'	1) 20 'Stayers' 28 'Movers' 2) 28 'Movers' (all adults)	Social indicators Lifestyle: personal life satisfaction Lifestyle: presence Lifestyle: participation Lifestyle: competence Lifestyle: choice	Community Settings: more 'normalized'; greater user satisfaction with lifestyle; no difference in frequency of community activities, more activities in integrated settings; more activity, more contact with friends and relatives, possible improvements in eating behaviour and reduction in neutral behaviours; no differences pre vs. post-move in 'movers' adaptive or maladaptive behaviour, 'movers' less maladaptive behaviour than 'stayers' at all times; greater independence and choice.
Booth et al (1990)	1) Mental Handicap Hospital 2) Community Hostels	Longitudinal	1) 16 adults 2) 16 adults	Social indicators Lifestyle: presence Lifestyle: participation Lifestyle: competence Lifestyle: choice Service processes Staff contact	Community Hostels: staff report more user time in community activities, users report more positive community relationships; users report increased domestic occupation, staff report that users lack social interaction; staff reported increased user confidence, independence, maturity, families report increased self-help and communication skills; users report more privacy and choice; staff report that users are lacking essential services; families report more staff attention.

62

Study	Settings	Design	Numbers	Domains Measured	Summary of Results
Bratt & Johnston (1988)	1) Mental Handicap Hospital 2) Community Staffed House	Longitudinal (post-move data collected at 2 time points)	1) 5 adults 2) 5 adults	Lifestyle: presence Lifestyle: engagement Service processes	Community Staffed House: more trips out of home, more trips to integrated community settings; gradual increase in user interaction with others, no difference in appropriate and neutral activities, less inappropriate activity; less visits from others (mainly professionals), but visitors stayed longer.
Cattermole et al (1988)	1) Community Hostels	n/a (retrospective interviews)	1) 12 adults	Lifestyle: participation Lifestyle: choice	Retrospective on pre-move situation (parental homes): almost all contact with family members, little integrated social activity, no friends without disabilities, little use of self-help skills; limited autonomy and choice. People active in the decision to move, more involved in pre-move integrated social activities and use of self-help skills, wanted more freedom and to get married in future.
Clare & Murphy (1993)	1) Mental Handicap Hospital 2) MIETS assessment and treatment unit for people with challenging behaviour 3) Community Staffed Houses	Longitudinal	1) 6 adults (T1) 2) 6 adults (T2) 3) 6 adults (T3)	Lifestyle: personal life satisfaction Lifestyle: presence Lifestyle: participation Lifestyle: competence Lifestyle: choice	Users prefer T3 service to T1 service (wide variation); increase in community-based activities T1-T2, not always maintained T2-T3; increased opportunities for domestic activities, increase in structured day-time activities T1-T2 & T3; reduction in total ABS scores T1-T3 for 2 users, reduction in referred challenging behaviour T1-T3 for 5 users; increase in socialization 5 users, communication 3 users, daily living skills 3 users T1-T3; privacy: 6 users shared bedrooms T1, 6 users single bedrooms T2, 3 users shared bedrooms, 3 users single bedrooms T3.

Study	Settings	Design	Numbers	Domains Measured	Summary of Results
Conneally et al (1992)	1) Community Hostel 2) Community Staffed Houses	Longitudinal (post-move data collected at 2 time points)	1) 11 adults 2) 11 adults	Social indicators Lifestyle: presence Lifestyle: engagement Lifestyle: participation Lifestyle: competence Carer outcomes Staff contact	Community staffed houses: more normalised in appearance, users more personal possessions; increase in number and variety of outings; increase in appropriate behaviour, decrease in inappropriate and neutral behaviour; increase in variety of in-home leisure activities; increase in adaptive behaviour, decrease in maladaptive behaviour; strongly preferred by families of users; no difference in levels of user interaction with staff or other users.
Cullen et al (in press)	1) Mental Handicap Hospital 2) Community Staffed Houses	Mixed Design: a) Longitudinal (data collected at 7 time points post-move) b) Comparison group 'Movers' vs. matched 'Stayers'	1) 50 'Stayers' 50 'Movers' 2) 50 'Movers' (all adults)	Social indicators Lifestyle: personal life satisfaction Lifestyle: presence Lifestyle: participation Lifestyle: competence Staff contact	Community staffed houses: no difference in user personal appearance, improvement in quality of physical environment; improvement in life satisfaction for movers T2-T5 (for stayers T2-T4); improvements in global quality of life measure; limited improvement in community living skills; no differences in adaptive behaviour (Part I ABS); increase in maladaptive behaviour (Part II ABS); more improvement in social skills; improvement in staff/user interactions, but interactions still very low for all users.
Dalgleish & Matthews (1980)	1) 2 Day Centres	n/a	1) 73 adults	Lifestyle: engagement Staff contact	For both day centres: more user engagement and staff/user interaction in craft zones than in halls, more user engagement and staff/user interaction in enclosed craft rooms than in open craft zones.

Study	Settings	Design	Numbers	Domains Measured	Summary of Results
Dalgleish & Matthews (1981)	1) 2 Day Centres	n/a	1) 73 adults	Lifestyle: engagement	For both day centres: stronger relationship between group size and user engagement than between staff ratios and user engagement.
Davies (1988)	1) Mental Handicap Hospital 2) Health Authority Community Staffed Houses 3) Social Services Community Staffed Houses 4) Private Community Hostels 5) Voluntary Agency Community Staffed House	Comparison groups	1) 25 adults 2) 17 adults 3) 14 adults 4) 46 adults 5) 8 adults	Lifestyle: participation Service processes Costs	Health authority and social services staffed houses higher in overall user quality of life, staff/user ratios, than other services; All community services less shared bedrooms than mental handicap hospital; Revenue costs per person per year (1986/87 prices): health authority houses £15,526-£23,394, social services houses £10,061-£13,520, private sector hostels £8,752-£12,314, voluntary agency house £12,354, mental handicap hospital £13,980. Large variations in staff costs across & within service types, some evidence for economies of scale.
Davies et al (1991)	1) Intensively Staffed Community Houses 2) Minimally Staffed Community House 3) Small Community Houses 4) Support Services To People Living With Parents	Comparison groups	1) approx 35 adults 2) 3 adults 3) 4 adults 4) n not given	Costs	Residential costs per person per year (1986/87 prices): minimally staffed house £7,393, other staffed houses £16,473-£23,319. Total costs per person per year (1986/87 prices): minimally staffed house £9,678, other staffed houses £21,708 (£18,883-£26,009). Most variation in staffing costs. Capital costs £13,129-£21,656 per place. Family home support costs £5,614. Comparing with other studies: no economy of scale, no link between costs and quality of service.

Study	Settings	Design	Numbers	Domains Measured	Summary of Results
de Kock et al (1988)	Two studies. Study 1 1) Mental Handicap Hospital 2) Community Staffed Houses Study 2 1) Community Units (25 beds) 2) Community Staffed Houses	Study 1: longitudinal Study 2: comparison groups	Study 1: 1) 10 adults 2) 10 adults Study 2: 1) 24 adults 2) 12 adults	Lifestyle: presence Lifestyle: participation	Study 1: more community and family contacts community staffed houses vs. mental handicap hospital. Study 2: more community contacts, trend for more family contacts community staffed houses vs. large community units.
Dockrell et al (1993)	1) Various pre-move services (7 users prison, 9 private/special hospitals, 13 mental handicap hospitals, 5 other) 2) MIETS assessment and treatment unit for people with challenging behaviour 3) Post-MIETS services (1 user prison, 7 private/special hospitals, 3 mental handicap hospitals, 3 hospital homes, 7 campus homes, 7 community homes, 5 own/parental home)	Longitudinal	1) 34 adults 2) 34 adults 3) 34 adults	Lifestyle: presence Lifestyle: participation Lifestyle: choice Carer outcomes Costs	Keyworkers in post-MIETS services report: hospitals; low access to neighbourhood, low use of community facilities, medium participation in domestic activities, low privacy, low choice, medium freedom; campus homes; medium access, high community use, high participation in domestic activities, low privacy, high choice, medium freedom; community homes; high access, high community use, high participation in domestic activities, high privacy, high choice, high freedom. Post-MIETS care staff and managers report a generally positive assessment of MIETS and a reduction in user challenging behaviours. Comprehensive costs per person per year (1989/90 prices): Prison £25,000, private hospital £52,000, special hospital £44,300, mental handicap hospital £32,000, MIETS £80,000, hospital home £27,000, campus home £36,000, community home £64,000.

Study	Settings	Design	Numbers	Domains Measured	Summary of Results
Donegan & Potts (1988)	1) Unstaffed residential accommodation for people living alone	n/a	1) 9 adults	Social indicators Lifestyle: presence Lifestyle: participation Lifestyle: choice	Accommodation same as surroundings, but in poor state of repair. 7 users reasonable number of working household goods. All users local shops, post office and pub; 8 users frequent bus service to shopping centre. Little integration, few activities outside home, little contact with friends. 6 users had hobbies (restricted due to finance), 8 users narrow range of activities, men narrower range of activities than women. Few visitors except support staff. 7 users had a high degree of autonomy over their lives.
Durward & Whatmore (1976)	1) Community Residential Unit C 2) Community Residential Unit E	Comparison group	1) 21 children 2) 31 children	Lifestyle: engagement Staff contact	Unit E: child appropriate behaviour more likely to be followed by staff contact. Mobile child appropriate behaviour more likely to be followed by staff contact than non-mobile child appropriate behaviour.
Emerson et al (1992)	1) Mental Handicap Hospital 2) Hospital-Based Staffed Houses for People with Challenging Behaviour	Mixed Design: a) longitudinal for 4 service users; b) 4 service users post-move only	1) 4 adults 2) 8 adults	Lifestyle: engagement Service processes Staff contact	Staffed House (longitudinal group): constructive activity dropped slightly for 3 users, increased slightly for 1 user; no difference in major challenging behaviours, reduction in minor challenging behaviours; improvement in actual and observed staff ratios; increase in user time unattended, increase in overall staff contact (mostly due to increase for 1 user).

67

Study	Settings	Design	Numbers	Domains Measured	Summary of Results
Emerson et al (1993)	1) Variety of pre-move services (10 users adult services, 6 users special education services) 2) Specialised Residential Unit for People with Learning Disabilities and Sensory Impairments	Longitudinal	1) 16 adults 2) 16 adults	Lifestyle: presence Lifestyle: engagement Lifestyle: participation Lifestyle: competence Carer outcomes Service processes Staff contact Costs	Specialised Residential Unit: overall no difference in community involvement, trend for decrease in community involvement compared to pre-move special education; overall higher user engagement, communication, less minor CB compared to pre-move special education, more engagement, communication compared to pre-move adult services; overall decrease in scheduled out-of-home activities, decrease compared to special education, no difference compared to adult services; overall increase in adaptive behaviour, less improvement compared to pre-move special education than compared to pre-move adult services; parents very satisfied; staff turnover twice as high as local learning disability services, staff report high levels of job satisfaction and stress; overall less contact with health professionals, less services reported as needed by staff; overall less social distance, more block treatment compared to pre-move special education, less social distance compared to pre-move adult services; overall more staff care, assistance, negative contact, staff/user communication, more care compared to pre-move special education, more staff contact, assistance, care, staff/user communication compared to pre-move adult services; increase in average weekly comprehensive costs, large variation in pre-move costs, no relationship between costs and quality.

Study	Settings	Design	Numbers	Domains Measured	Summary of Results
Evans et al (1985)	1) Mental Handicap Hospital 2) Community Staffed House	Longitudinal	1) 4 adults 2) 4 adults	Lifestyle: presence Lifestyle: engagement Staff contact	Community Staffed House: 2 users more time in community; 2 users increased social & domestic activity, 1 user decreased eating, drinking, recreational activity; 3 users increased contact with staff.
Felce (1981)	1) Mental Handicap Hospital 1 (large campus-style) 2) Mental Handicap Hospital 2 (smaller campus-style) 3) Community Residential Unit	Comparison groups	n/a Focus of study on capital costs.	Costs	Actual Capital Expenditure per place (1978 prices): Hospital 1 £17,735 compared to equivalent Community Residential Units £12,319; Hospital 2 £16,335 compared to equivalent Community Residential Units £15,657. No economies of scale.

Study	Settings	Design	Numbers	Domains Measured	Summary of Results
Felce (1989)	1) Mental Handicap Hospital 2) Large Community Unit 3) Family Home 4) Community Staffed House	Longitudinal and Comparison Groups	1) Not given 2) Not given 3) Not given 4) 14 adults NB: publication summarises results from several studies	Lifestyle: presence Lifestyle: engagement Lifestyle: participation Lifestyle: competence Lifestyle: social status Carer outcomes Staff contact Costs	Community Staffed Houses: more use of community facilities, more family contact compared to large community units and mental handicap hospitals; increased (and more varied) user engagement compared to large community units and mental handicap hospitals (maintained 2 years post-move); large increase in adaptive behaviours, smaller increase for people in family homes, no increase people in mental handicap hospitals; high degree of acceptance from local businesses (shops, cafes, pubs) frequented by people in community staffed houses; staff turnover much higher compared to mental handicap hospitals; more overall staff contact, instruction and guidance compared to large community units and mental handicap hospitals; people with greatest handicaps receive more staff support; strong relationship between level of staff support and level of resident engagement; group size more important influence on staff contact than staff ratios. Capital costs (per place): staffed houses £14,500-£17,500; large community units £13,400-£17,150. Revenue costs (per person per day, 1984/85 prices): staffed houses £41.87, large community units £31.04, mental handicap hospitals £37.03.

Study	Settings	Design	Numbers	Domains Measured	Summary of Results
Felce (1994)	1) Community Staffed House	n/a	1) 57 adults	Lifestyle: engagement Staff contact	Across all houses, average user engagement 49%. User engagement increased with user ability. Levels of user engagement (controlling for resident ability) lower than in staffed housing service reported in Felce (1989). Across all houses, average staff contact 27%. Only 15% of staff contact is assistance.
Felce & Repp (1992)	1) Mental Handicap Hospital 2) Large Community Unit 3) Community Staffed House	Comparison Groups	1) 40 adults 2) 30 adults 3) 20 adults	Lifestyle: engagement Staff contact	Larger group size associated with less user engagement and staff interaction. Most user engagement and staff interaction when users are in groups supervised by one or two staff.
Felce et al (1986a)	1) Mental Handicap Hospital 2) Community Staffed House	Mixed design: a) Longitudinal for 6 users, b) Comparison Groups for 6 users in community staffed house	1) 6 adults 2) 12 adults	Lifestyle: engagement Staff contact	User appropriate activity higher, neutral behaviour lower in community staffed houses than in mental handicap hospitals. Longitudinal study: no difference in user inappropriate activity pre- vs. post-move. Higher durations and rates of staff contact in community staffed houses than in mental handicap hospitals.

Study	Settings	Design	Numbers	Domains Measured	Summary of Results
Felce et al (1986b)	Time 1: 8 people mental handicap hospitals, 10 people community staffed houses, 10 people parental homes; Time 2 (T1+18 months): 8 people mental handicap hospitals, 8 people community staffed houses, 10 people parental homes; Time 3 (T1+36 months): 4 people mental handicap hospitals, 12 people community staffed houses, 10 people parental homes.	Longitudinal	1) 28 adults 2) 26 adults 3) 26 adults	Lifestyle: competence	Overall increase in adaptive behaviour T1-T3. Increase in adaptive behaviour greater for staffed house group than for parental home group and mental handicap hospital group.
Felce et al (1980)	1) Mental Handicap Hospital 2) Large Community Units	Comparison Groups	1) 43 children 119 adults 2) 77 children 24 adults	Lifestyle: engagement	Higher levels of child and adult engagement, lower levels of disengagement, in large community units than in mental handicap hospitals.

72

Study	Settings	Design	Numbers	Domains Measured	Summary of Results
Felce et al (1994)	1) Mental Handicap Hospital 2) Parental Home 3) Community Staffed House	Longitudinal (pre-move mental handicap hospital & parental home; post-move community staffed house)	1) 32 adults 2) 4 adults 3) 36 adults	Lifestyle: presence Lifestyle: engagement Lifestyle: competence	Community Staffed Houses: increased community and family contact compared to mental handicap hospitals; increase in user engagement and challenging behaviour compared to mental handicap hospitals; increase in adaptive behaviour and skills compared to mental handicap hospitals.
Felce et al (1991)	1) Mental Handicap Hospital 2) Large Community Unit 3) Community Staffed House	Comparison Groups	1) 40 adults 2) 30 adults 3) 20 adults	Lifestyle: engagement Staff contact	Community Staffed Houses: users spend less time alone compared to large community units and mental handicap hospitals; staff work alone more, less frequent large user group sizes, compared to large community units and mental handicap hospitals. Small group sizes, highest levels of user appropriate behaviour and staff interaction.
Felce et al (1987)	1) Mental Handicap Hospital 2) Large Community Unit 3) Community Staffed House	Comparison Groups	1) 40 adults 2) 30 adults 3) 20 adults	Lifestyle: engagement Staff contact	Community Staffed Houses: more staff encouragement of appropriate user behaviour, more neutral and discouraging staff responses to inappropriate user behaviour, compared to large units and mental handicap hospitals.

73

Study	Settings	Design	Numbers	Domains Measured	Summary of Results
Felce et al (1985)	1) Mental Handicap Hospital 2) Community Staffed House	Mixed Design: a) longitudinal hospital-house for 6 users; b) comparison groups for 6 users post-move only	1) 6 adults 2) 12 adults	Lifestyle: social indicators Lifestyle: engagement Lifestyle: choice	Community Staffed Houses: materially enriched compared to mental handicap hospitals; users spent more time engaged with a greater variety of material items compared to mental handicap hospitals; all functional areas open to free access by users, compared to restricted access for users in mental handicap hospitals.
Fleming & Stenfert Kroese (1990)	1) Mental Handicap Hospital 2) Community Hostel 3) Community Staffed House	Longitudinal (services 1 & 2 pre-move, service 3 post-move)	1) 9 adults 2) 8 adults 3) 17 adults	Lifestyle: presence Lifestyle: participation Lifestyle: competence Lifestyle: choice	Community Staffed Houses: user outings frequent during day, infrequent in evening, more able users have more outings; most visitors service-related, few visits from friends; overall increase in skills compared to pre-move services, biggest increase in household skills, users in houses with goal planning showed more improvement than users in houses without goal planning; user decision-making marginally increased compared to pre-move services, still below normative.

Study	Settings	Design	Numbers	Domains Measured	Summary of Results
Flynn (1989)	1) Independent Living	n/a	1) 88 adults	Lifestyle: social indicators Lifestyle: personal life satisfaction Lifestyle: presence Lifestyle: participation Lifestyle: competence Lifestyle: choice Lifestyle: social status Service processes	Employment status: 12 people open employment, 29 attend day services, 20 retired, 27 unemployed or looking for work. 55 people income less than £55 weekly. Majority of people in council housing. Over half have a washing machine, over a quarter have a telephone. 5 people wanted a higher income. 17 people wanted to move house. 38 people have regular (but not always positive) contact with neighbours. 26 people living alone, 37 with one other person (9 couples), 25 with two or more other people. 33 people have regular, 23 intermittent, contact with relatives. People largely accomplished in using public transport, dressing appropriately, maintaining proper sleep habits; need more help in managing finances, paying bills, handling medical problems. Mostly people's living arrangements reflect their active preferences. 29 people report victimization from local people. 46 people have at least weekly contact with social worker, reliance on social worker for help with finance and medical problems. Social workers treat users as independent adults, report independence as an objective for 41 users.

75

Study	Settings	Design	Numbers	Domains Measured	Summary of Results
Hemming (1986)	1) Mental Handicap Hospital 2) Hospital-Based Residential Unit	Mixed Design: a) Longitudinal (hospital-unit), data collected at 5 points post-move (up to 5.5 years) b) Comparison Groups ('movers' vs. 'stayers' in hospital)	a) 29 adult 'movers' b) 29 adult 'stayers'	Lifestyle: competence	Residential Unit: high ability residents, higher domestic activity & total ABS score; low ability residents, higher independent functioning, domestic activity, responsibility, socialization, total ABS score; 5.5. years post-move vs. pre-move (hospital). No change in language ability post-move vs. pre-move. No difference between Movers and Stayers on ABS scores.
Hemming et al (1981)	1) Mental Handicap Hospital 2) Hospital-Based Residential Unit	Mixed Design: a) Longitudinal (hospital-unit), data collected at 4 points post-move (up to 2 years) b) Comparison Groups ('movers' vs. 'stayers' in hospital)	a) 38 adult 'movers' b) 33 adult 'stayers'	Lifestyle: presence Lifestyle: engagement Lifestyle: participation Lifestyle: competence Service processes Staff contact	Residential Unit: decreased daytime occupation off-site compared to mental handicap hospital, few nonroutine activities pre- or post-move; no differences in user training and caring activities, less user disengagement from activities compared to mental handicap hospital; more user domestic activity, no change in on-site daytime activities, compared to mental handicap hospital; post-move improvement in Part I ABS scores peaks at 9 months, at 2 years post-move improvements in domestic activity, self-direction, total Part I ABS score; little change in ABS maladaptive behaviour, except for post-move increase in self-abusive behaviour; less block treatment, depersonalization, social distance, total institutionalization, compared to mental handicap hospitals; more staff interactions of better quality compared to mental handicap hospitals.

Study	Settings	Design	Numbers	Domains Measured	Summary of Results
Hewson & Walker (1992)	1) Community Staffed Houses	n/a	1) 59 adults	Lifestyle: presence Lifestyle: engagement Lifestyle: participation Lifestyle: competence Service processes Staff contact	Mean waking hours outside house 20.9% (11.3% excluding SEC attendance); mean user constructive engagement 49.96%; mean waking hours spent with visitors 8.1%; mean user disturbed behaviour 14.86%, most frequent self-stimulation/stereotypy, self injury & inappropriate vocalisation; written statement of service aims, written IPPs for every user, weekly staff meetings, key worker for every user, staff appraisal; each of these only in place in 1 house out of 10; mean staff contact 21.14%, less than 10% of contact active staff assistance.
Hoefkens & Allen (1990)	1) Various pre-move services (32 admissions to service): 15 mental handicap hospital, 9 parental home, 5 community staffed house, 2 hostel, 1 secure hospital 2) Hospital-Based Special Behaviour Unit 3) Various post-move services: 7 to parental home, 6 to mental handicap hospital, 3 to community staffed houses (6 people still in service 2)	Longitudinal	1) 16 adults 2) 16 adults 3) 16 adults	Lifestyle: competence Service processes	Data presented on challenging behaviour for 4 users: pre-move – unit: 3 users decrease, 1 user no change, in challenging behaviour; unit – post-move: 4 users increase in challenging behaviour. 119 service interventions in 15 months, mostly least restrictive.

Study	Settings	Design	Numbers	Domains Measured	Summary of Results
Hughes & Mansell (1990)	1) Community Staffed House 2) Day Service	n/a (users were living in staffed houses and attending day services)	1) 45 adults 2) 45 adults	Lifestyle: engagement Staff contact	Community Staffed House and Day Service: levels of user engagement and challenging behaviour low; little staff contact, majority of contact neutral interaction.
Jahoda et al (1990)	1) Hospital Leavers (mental handicap hospital to community hostel) 2) Home Leavers (parental home to community hostel) 3) Home Stayers (parental home)	n/a (retrospective interviews with users and carers)	1) 8 adults 2) 7 adults 3) 10 adults	Lifestyle: personal life satisfaction Lifestyle: presence Lifestyle: participation	Hospital Leavers: 4 users report improvement in life satisfaction, 4 no change; decrease in special and ordinary activities; increase in semi-integrative and integrative activities; most social contacts with other people with learning disabilities; less contact with family at all times than other groups. Home Leavers: 5 users report improvement in life satisfaction, 2 no change; increased semi-integrative and integrative activities; increased contact with other people with learning disabilities. Home Stayers: all 10 users report no change in life satisfaction; no change in activities.
Joyce et al (1989)	1) Community Staffed House	n/a	1) 3 adults	Lifestyle: engagement Lifestyle: participation	Direct observation of user engagement more reliable than diaries of user activity. Less agreement between methods with more active service users.

Study	Settings	Design	Numbers	Domains Measured	Summary of Results
Knapp et al (1992)	1) Mental Handicap Hospital 2) Various community pilot projects (community hostels, staffed houses, independent living)	Mixed Design: a) Longitudinal 196 'Movers' b) Comparison Groups 373 'Stayers'	1) 569 adults 2) 196 adults	Lifestyle: personal life satisfaction Lifestyle: participation Lifestyle: competence Costs	Community Pilot Projects: increase in user satisfaction with services and overall life satisfaction compared to pre-move and stayers; no change in contact with friends and family compared to pre-move and stayers; increase in user skills compared to pre-move and stayers, larger skills increase in community staffed houses than in community hostels; no change in maladaptive user behaviour compared to pre-move and stayers, more maladaptive user behaviour in community hostels than in community staffed houses. Costs: mixed results, some community placements more expensive than mental handicap hospitals, some cheaper.
Locker et al (1984)	1) Mental Handicap Hospital 2) Parental Home 3) Community Hostel	Comparison Groups (data collected on each group at 4 time points over 12 months)	1) 8 adults 2) 12 adults 3) 17 adults	Lifestyle: competence	Users in community hostels show steady improvement in adaptive behaviour over 12 months. Users in parental home show little improvement in adaptive behaviour (except for socialization) over 12 months. Users in mental handicap hospital show little improvement in adaptive behaviour over 9 months, improve in final 3 months. Users in community hostels show larger improvements in adaptive behaviour than users in parental homes and mental handicap hospitals.

79

Study	Settings	Design	Numbers	Domains Measured	Summary of Results
Lowe & de Paiva (1990)	Data from 2 studies: a) 1) Mental Handicap Hospital 2) Parental Home 3) Community Staffed House 4) Parental Home (with additional support) 5) Mental Handicap Hospital (with additional support) b) 1) Parental Home 2) Mental Handicap Hospital	Mixed Design: a) Longitudinal (users from services 1 and 2 transferred to service 3) and Comparison Groups b) Comparison Groups (in both studies data collected at 8 time points over 5 years)	a) 1) 22 adults 2) 5 adults 3) 27 adults 4) 35 adults 5) 30 adults b) 1) 10 adults 2) 14 adults	Lifestyle: competence	(Part I ABS) Largest increase in adaptive behaviour over 5 years for users living in community staffed houses (service a3), smaller but significant increase over 5 years for users living in parental homes with additional support (service a4). (Pathways to Independence) Increase in independence over 5 years for users living in community staffed houses (service a3), no significant change for any other group.
Lowe & de Paiva (1991)	Data from 2 studies: a) 1) Mental Handicap Hospital 2) Parental Home 3) Community Staffed House 4) Parental Home (with additional support) 5) Mental Handicap Hospital (with additional support) b) 1) Parental Home 2) Mental Handicap Hospital	Mixed Design: a) Longitudinal (users from services 1 and 2 transferred to service 3) and Comparison Groups b) Comparison Groups (in both studies data collected at 8 time points over 5 years)	a) 1) 22 adults 2) 5 adults 3) 27 adults 4) 35 adults 5) 30 adults b) 1) 10 adults 2) 14 adults	Lifestyle: presence Lifestyle: participation	Use of community facilities increased over 5 years for users in community staffed houses (service a3), parental homes with additional support (service a4) and parental homes with no additional support (service b1), most used facilities parks, shops, cafes. Use of community facilities no change over 5 years for users in mental handicap hospitals (services a5 and b2), most used facilities parks. Little contact with friends all users living in residential accommodation (services a3, a5, b2), some evidence for increase for users in community staffed houses (service a3) up to levels for users in parental homes (services a4 and b1). Little contact with family (and no change over time) for all users living in residential accommodation (services a3, a5, b2).

Study	Settings	Design	Numbers	Domains Measured	Summary of Results
Lowe et al (1992)	1) Day Centre 1 (ATC) 2) Day Centre 2 (SEC)	Comparison Groups	1) 145 places 2) 59 places	Lifestyle: engagement Lifestyle: participation Staff contact	Day Centre 1: more timetabled activities in arts and crafts, work experience compared to Day Centre 2; less timetabled activities in personal development, volunteering compared to Day Centre 2; similar levels of user engagement compared to Day Centre 2. Majority of staff behaviour direct contact with service users in both Day Centres.
Lowe et al (1993)	Data from 2 studies: a) 1) Mental Handicap Hospital 2) Parental Home 3) Community Staffed House 4) Parental Home (with additional support) 5) Mental Handicap Hospital (with additional support) b) 1) Parental Home 2) Mental Handicap Hospital	Mixed Design: a) Longitudinal (users from services 1 and 2 transferred to service 3) and Comparison Groups b) Comparison Groups (in both studies data collected at 8 time points over 5 years)	a) 1) 22 adults 2) 5 adults 3) 27 adults 4) 35 adults 5) 30 adults b) 1) 10 adults 2) 14 adults	Lifestyle: competence	(Part I ABS) Largest increase in adaptive behaviour over 5 years for users living in community staffed houses (service a3), smaller but significant increase over 5 years for users living in parental homes with additional support (service a4). (Pathways to Independence) Increase in independence over 5 years for users living in community staffed houses (service a3), no significant change for any other group. (DAS) Increase in maladaptive behaviour over 5 years for users living in community staffed houses (service a3), no significant change for any other group.

Study	Settings	Design	Numbers	Domains Measured	Summary of Results
Malin (1982)	1) Community Staffed House	n/a	1) 24 adults	Lifestyle: presence Lifestyle: participation	21 (out of 24) residents reported knowing 1 or more neighbours, reported 2 or less friends (excluding co-residents and workmates), with infrequent (monthly or less) contact. Users reported having an average of 4 relatives, with an average 2.3 relatives per resident being in contact (most frequently brothers and sisters). 5 residents had no contact with relatives.
Mansell & Beasley (1990)	1) Mental Handicap Hospital 2) Mental Handicap Hospital – Secure Ward 3) Hospital-Based Campus Unit 4) Community Staffed House	Mixed Design: a) Longitudinal (4 users moving from services 1, 2 and 3 into service 4) b) Comparison Groups (services 1, 2 and 3)	Services 1, 2 & 3: 18 adults Service 4: 4 adults	Lifestyle: engagement Staff contact	Community Staffed House: 2 users showed clear increase in engagement compared to pre-move services, 2 showed no difference in engagement. 2 users in hospital throughout the study showed no difference in engagement over time. Higher levels of staff contact in community staffed houses than in all other settings. This increase attributable to increase in neutral staff contact and staff assistance.

Study	Settings	Design	Numbers	Domains Measured	Summary of Results
Mansell & Beasley (1993)	1) Mental Handicap Hospital 2) Mental Handicap Hospital – Secure Ward 3) Hospital-Based Campus Unit 4) Community Staffed House	Longitudinal (7 people transferred from mental handicap hospital to campus unit) (11 people transferred from mental handicap hospital to community staffed house) Data collected at 7 points over 3 years	1) 10 adults 2) 8 adults 3) 7 adults 4) 11 adults	Lifestyle: engagement Staff contact	For 11 users moving from mental handicap hospital to community staffed house: overall increase in appropriate user activity, 10 users showed big increases immediately post-move, 3 users immediate post-move increase not sustained; no overall change in user problem behaviour post-move, but general post-move decrease in self-stimulatory behaviour. Overall staff contact, direct staff assistance, higher in community staffed houses than in mental handicap hospitals and campus units
Mansell et al (1984)	1) Community Staffed House	n/a	1) 6 adults	Lifestyle: engagement	All users, substantial proportions of time spent in kitchen, utility room and living room. 3 users over 50% appropriate activity, 3 users approx. 20% appropriate activity. For all users, over 25% of appropriate activity spent in domestic activity. 4 users, relatively large proportion of time spent in inappropriate activity.

83

Study	Settings	Design	Numbers	Domains Measured	Summary of Results
Markova et al (1992)	1) Mental Handicap Hospital 2) Community Hostel	Comparison Groups	1) 12 adults 2) 12 adults	Lifestyle: participation	More interactions overall in community hostels, more functional interactions in mental handicap hospitals. More friendly attitudes from staff and co-residents in community hostels, more impersonal, ignoring and controlling interactions from co-residents and staff in mental handicap hospitals. In both settings, over 95% of interactions are less than 4 minutes long.
Martindale & Kilby (1982)	1) Mental Handicap Hospital 2) Various Post-Move Services (Old Mental Handicap Hospitals, New Mental Handicap Hospitals, New Hospital Hostels)	Longitudinal (data collection pre-move, post-move, post-move+3 years)	1) 83 adults 2) 61 adults (16 old hospitals, 24 new hospitals, 21 new hospital hostels)	Lifestyle: participation Lifestyle: competence	Increase in education/training/employment post-move for users moving to new hospitals and hospital hostels. No long-term change in contact with relatives for any user group. Long-term improvement in incontinence problems all groups, no change in self-help skills hospital hostel group, long-term deterioration in self-help skills other user groups. No long-term change in behaviour problems for any user group.

Study	Settings	Design	Numbers	Domains Measured	Summary of Results
McConkey et al (1993)	Study focuses on community acceptance rather than service users. 2 groups of people: 1) people living close to where community staffed houses were going to open (data collected pre- and post-opening) 2) people in comparable areas with no service opening	Mixed Design: a) longitudinal (before and after service opens; b) comparison groups (people near services vs. people not near services)	1) T1, 148 adults T2, 145 adults 2) T1, 94 adults T2, 83 adults	Lifestyle: presence Lifestyle: social status	Increase in neighbours' contacts with people with learning disabilities post-opening compared to pre-opening and control group. Drop in number of perceived problems, increase in perceived benefits of service, post-opening compared to pre-opening and control group. Drop in neighbours' stated willingness to help post-opening compared to pre-opening and control group (due to social desirability factors).
McGill et al (1994)	1) Mental Handicap Hospital 2) Community Staffed House	Longitudinal	1) 11 adults 2) 11 adults	Lifestyle: engagement Staff contact Costs	Community Staffed Houses: increased user constructive activity compared to mental handicap hospitals; 9 users reduced or same level of minor problem behaviours, 9 users reduced or same level of major problem behaviours, compared to mental handicap hospitals; increased staff interaction and assistance compared to mental handicap hospitals; average revenue cost (1991/92 prices) per person per year: community staffed houses £53,000.

Study	Settings	Design	Numbers	Domains Measured	Summary of Results
McHatton et al (1988)	1) Mental Handicap Hospital 2) Hospital-Based Residential Unit	Longitudinal	1) 6 adults 2) 6 adults	Lifestyle: presence Lifestyle: engagement Lifestyle: participation Lifestyle: competence Lifestyle: choice Staff contact	Hospital-Based Residential Unit (compared to Mental Handicap Hospital): no change in number of out-of-home trips; increase in user appropriate activity, decrease in user inappropriate activity; increase in the number of variety of domestic tasks carried out by users; overall increase in user skills; increase in user choice and independence; increase in staff:resident contact, no change in resident:staff contact, trend towards decrease in resident:resident contact.
Murphy & Clare (1991)	1) Mental Handicap Hospital 2) Mental Handicap Hospital – Secure Ward 3) MIETS assessment and treatment unit for people with challenging behaviour	Longitudinal (users moved from services 1 & 2 to service 3) Data collection immediately after admission to MIETS and just before discharge from MIETS	1) 3 adults 2) 3 adults 3) 6 adults	Lifestyle: competence	All 6 users improved in daily living and socialization skills, 4 users improved in communication skills. General decrease in maladaptive behaviour (Part II ABS) throughout time at MIETS, but some users show increase just before discharge from MIETS.

Study	Settings	Design	Numbers	Domains Measured	Summary of Results
Murphy et al (1991)	1) Various pre-move services (2 users special hospital, 11 mental handicap hospital, 3 prison, 3 community staffed houses) 2) MIETS assessment and treatment unit for people with challenging behaviour	Longitudinal	1) 19 adults 2) 19 adults	Lifestyle: presence Lifestyle: choice Carer outcomes Staff contact	One violent incident in community in 18 months of MIETS operation. MIETS locked approx. 15% of day time hours, seclusion used 84 times in 18 months (average 3.5 duration). Care staff more optimistic, more involved in decision-making than staff in comparative studies working in mental handicap hospitals. 86% of staff:user interactions 'accepting', 14% 'tolerating', 1% 'rejecting', more accepting interactions than comparative studies in psychiatric day centres and hostels.
Orlowska et al (1991)	1) Community Staffed House	n/a	1) 6 adults	Staff contact	71.7% of staff time spent interacting with users. When staff are with users, 79.1% staff time spent interacting with users. More staff:resident interaction in small staff groups.
Pettipher & Mansell (1993)	1) Community Day Service	n/a	1) 33 adults	Lifestyle: engagement Staff contact	User activity: low ability group 22%, middle ability group 46%, high ability group 66%, time spent engaged; disengagement; low and middle ability group, most common code waiting for staff; high ability group, most common code inactive (spectating). Staff contact: low ability group 14%, middle ability group 9%, high ability group 5% time spent receiving staff contact.

Study	Settings	Design	Numbers	Domains Measured	Summary of Results
Rawlings (1985a)	1) Mental Handicap Hospital 2) Community Staffed House	Comparison Groups	1) 12 adults 2) 11 adults	Lifestyle: engagement Lifestyle: competence Service processes Staff contact	Community Staffed Houses (compared to mental handicap hospital): more user engagement, less user stereotypy; no difference in user self-help skills; staff have more management autonomy, less block treatment of users; more social staff:user contact.
Rawlings (1985b)	1) Mental Handicap Hospital 2) Community Staffed House	Comparison Groups	1) 12 adults 2) 11 adults	Lifestyle: engagement Lifestyle: competence Service processes Staff contact	Community Staffed Houses (compared to mental handicap hospital): more user engagement, less user stereotypy; no difference in user self-help skills; staff have more management autonomy, less block treatment of users; more social staff:user contact.
Saxby et al (1986)	1) Community Staffed House	n/a	1) 10 adults	Lifestyle: presence Lifestyle: engagement Lifestyle: social status	Contact with members of public: occurred for 9 users while shopping, 6 users in cafes/pubs; mean duration of contact very low (1.7% observed time). User appropriate behaviour 29.3% shops, 36.3% cafes/pubs. User inappropriate behaviour (shown by 7 users) 6.4% shops, 11.3% cafes/pubs, mostly stereotypy. Managers and workers in local shops/pubs/cafes: preferred groups of 2 users at a time, 32.4% said users stood out at least to a moderate degree, 45.9% said users stood out a little, 21.6% said user did not stand out at all. 87.6% said users as presentable as average customers. 34.2% said users' behaviour similar to others, 63.2% said users' behaviour reasonable considering handicap. 67% said users were an advantage for the business, 97.4% said users benefited from living in the community.

Study	Settings	Design	Numbers	Domains Measured	Summary of Results
Shiell et al (1992)	1) 123 Community Residential Facilities 59 local authority services (mean places 17.5) 41 health authority services (mean places 9.3) 59 private sector services (mean places 12.3) 33 voluntary sector services (mean places 9.5)	Comparison Groups	n/a (focus of study on service settings rather than individuals)	Lifestyle: competence Service processes Costs	Less user dependency in independent sector services compared to statutory sector services. More user dependency in health than local authority services. Staff:user ratios, proportion of qualified staff, higher in health authority services compared to other services. Salary costs per staff hour lower in health than in local authority services (no data from independent sector services) Mean costs across all facilities £38 per user day (range £16-£95). Overall independent sector services cheaper than statutory sector services. Association between higher user dependency and higher service costs. Controlling for user dependency, no relationship between size of facility and costs.
Sinson (1990)	1) Community Hostels (unified residential and day services) 2) Community Hostels (no unified residential and day services)	Comparison Groups	n/a (focus of study on service settings rather than individuals)	Service processes	Community hostels with unified programme across residential and day services showed superior management practices, better opportunities for neighbourhood co-ordination. All services showed a generally impoverished material environment.

Study	Settings	Design	Numbers	Domains Measured	Summary of Results
Stanley & Roy (1988)	1) Mental Handicap Hospital 2) Community Staffed House	Mixed Design: a) longitudinal (7 'Movers' from hospital to community) b) comparison groups (7 'Movers' vs. 7 'Stayers') (in addition, 100 local people without disabilities provided social validation of the measures)	1) 14 adults 2) 7 adults	Lifestyle: personal life satisfaction Lifestyle: presence Lifestyle: participation Lifestyle: competence Service processes	Community Staffed House: users higher levels of satisfaction than pre-move and stayers (rated by care staff), and similar levels of satisfaction to local community; no difference in use of community facilities compared to pre-move and stayers, lower use of community facilities than local community; higher scores on quality of life measure (rated by care staff) than pre-move and stayers, similar scores to local community; no difference in adaptive behaviours compared to pre-move and stayers; increased quality of care compared to pre-move and stayers.
Thomas et al (1986)	1) Mental Handicap Hospital 2) Large Community Unit 3) Community Staffed House	Comparison Groups	1) 20 adults 2) 20 adults 3) 10 adults	Lifestyle: engagement Staff contact	User engagement lowest in mental handicap hospitals, higher in community units, highest in community staffed houses. User:staff interaction higher in community staffed houses than in large community units and mental handicap hospitals. Inappropriate user activity highest in mental handicap hospitals, lower in community units, lowest in community staffed houses. Most staff contact in mental handicap hospitals and community units neutral (over 80%), lower proportion in community staffed houses (46%).

Study	Settings	Design	Numbers	Domains Measured	Summary of Results
Walker et al (1993)	1) Mental Handicap Hospital 2) Community Staffed House	Longitudinal	1) number not given 2) 62 adults	Social indicators Lifestyle: personal life satisfaction Lifestyle: participation Lifestyle: competence Lifestyle: choice Carer outcomes Service processes	Community Staffed Houses: accommodation superior to mental handicap hospitals; user disposable income varies according to district placement funding arrangements; preferred by 58 (out of 62) users (retrospective interview); families report improvement in relationships with users; staff report that users have an encouraging level of contact with neighbours in community staffed houses, but that users have few real friends, limited use of community facilities, and little meaningful day-time activity; staff report greater improvements in user basic living skills than in social skills; little involvement of service users in resettlement process, little choice over where to move, who to move with, contents of service package; families reported less concern resettlement post-move compared to pre-move, 95% reported positive aspects of resettlement, 33% reported negative aspects of resettlement; staff were all positive about resettlement; staffing levels inadequate to meet service aims, staff are unqualified, inexperienced, and require training; the majority of staff report unmet user needs.

Study	Settings	Design	Numbers	Domains Measured	Summary of Results
Wood (1989)	1) Mental Handicap Hospital Ward A 2) Mental Handicap Hospital Ward B (more progressive)	Comparison Groups	n/a (study focuses on staff rather than service users)	Lifestyle: engagement Staff contact	High level of neutral user behaviour in both wards. Staff Behaviour: Ward A: 39% staff/resident, 9% staff/staff, 52% no interaction. Most staff/resident interactions positive and verbal, occur average once per hour; Ward B: 41% staff/resident, 11% staff/staff, 48% no interaction. Most staff/resident interactions positive and verbal, occur average every 40 minutes. More informative or general talk from staff in Ward B than in Ward A.